FRBR

A Guide for the Perplexed

Robert L. Maxwell

American Library Association
Chicago   2008

While extensive effort has gone into ensuring the reliability of information appearing in this book, the publisher makes no warranty, express or implied, on the accuracy or reliability of the information, and does not assume and hereby disclaims any liability to any person for any loss or damage caused by errors or omissions in this publication.

Printed on 50-pound white offset, a pH-neutral stock, and bound in 10-point cover stock by Victor Graphics.

The paper used in this publication meets the minimum requirements of American National Standard for Information Sciences—Permanence of Paper for Printed Library Materials, ANSI Z39.48-1992. ∞

Library of Congress Cataloging-in-Publication Data
Maxwell, Robert L., 1957–
    FRBR : a guide for the perplexed / Robert L. Maxwell.
        p.   cm.
    Includes bibliographical references and index.
    ISBN 978-0-8389-0950-8 (alk. paper)
    1. FRBR (Conceptual model) I. Title.
    Z666.6.M39 2008
    025.3—dc22   2007027845

ISBN-13: 978-0-8389-0950-8
ISBN-10: 0-8389-0950-7

Printed in the United States of America

12   11   10   09   08   5   4   3   2   1

CONTENTS

ACKNOWLEDGMENTS

FRBR: A Guide for the Perplexed would not have been written without the cooperation of several individuals and organizations. First I must thank my employer, the Harold B. Lee Library, for a month's leave during the summer of 2006, which allowed me time to do research and study on FRBR. I am also grateful to my brother, Brian Maxwell, who helped me wrap my mind around the complexities of entities, relations, and attributes. Special thanks go to my patient editors at ALA Editions, who watched at least two deadlines pass without a manuscript and who helped make this book a better one than I could have written alone. And I especially thank my wife, Mary Ann Maxwell, and children, Carrie, Rachel, William, and David, for their unrelenting support at times when I was away writing and would rather have been with them. As always, this book is dedicated to them.

CHAPTER 1

Introduction

Functional Requirements for Bibliographic Records (FRBR) has been with us for nearly a decade, and few in the library world have not at least heard of it.[1] My experience speaking with colleagues in public services positions and even many in technical services positions has shown, however, that many librarians even now do not know what to make of it, and vendors of many library systems seem unconvinced. The purpose of this book is to explain and illustrate the FRBR model, show why the document and model are important for the future of information organization, and offer suggestions along the way for what a database founded on FRBR principles might look like.

What is FRBR? It is not a new code of cataloging rules—in fact, it claims to be code-neutral. It is not a database structure—it also purports to be system-neutral. Instead, the published document illustrates a new model of the bibliographic universe. That universe includes everything that libraries, bookstores, museums, and other similar entities might collect. It also includes all persons, bodies, or families that might interact with those collections in any way—as authors, as owners, as producers. It also includes all concepts that might be needed to describe other entities in the bibliographic universe. The model shows us ways these entities all interact with each other and ways users of libraries and other providers of bibliographic information interact with databases to obtain what they need. And it recommends a model that will go a long way toward helping untangle the explosion of information that is characteristic of the late twentieth and early twenty-first centuries.

FRBR sees itself as the culmination of a long tradition of cataloging theory beginning in the nineteenth century and including the 1961 Paris Principles,[2] the International Standard Bibliographic Description series (ISBDs) starting a decade later,[3] and the catalog codes that are based on them. The document was produced under the auspices of IFLA, the International Federation of Library Associations and Institutions, which was also the body that sponsored the production of the Paris Principles.

By the late 1980s many in the cataloging world, including members of the IFLA Section on Cataloguing, recognized that fundamental changes were happening in the environment that might require a rethinking of the way we conceive of and organize information. As summarized in the introduction to FRBR, these included

- the advent of automated systems, which prompted near-universal acceptance of the idea of shared cataloging and allowed advances in this area;
- the consequent rise of bibliographic utilities that were building vast databases of information about library resources;
- given that environment, a wish to minimize duplicate efforts;
- strongly expressed desires on the part of administrators and others to reduce cataloging costs that, despite immense savings brought on by the ability to share cataloging copy, continued to be perceived as overly expensive; and
- significant changes in the bibliographic universe itself, with the introduction of new formats, electronic publishing, and networked access (see FRBR 1.1, p. 1).

In 1990 a conference was held in Stockholm sponsored by the IFLA Universal Bibliographic Control and International MARC Programme and the IFLA Division of Bibliographic Control, at which these environmental changes were discussed.[4] The conference set several resolutions, one of which was to commission a study of the functions of the bibliographic record, with particular attention to be paid to user needs. It was hoped that such a study would provide a clear and commonly shared understanding of the purposes of the bibliographic record.

One of the expected outcomes of this study was an identification of the core components of the bibliographic record that could be agreed upon internationally. This was so that national bibliographic agencies could exchange records, using the work of others with little or no further intervention on their part. The agreed-upon core components were to be based, however, not on the convenience of the cataloger or on perceived pressure to reduce costs but on the needs of users of the records. Specifically, the study would

1. Determine in full the functions of the bibliographic record and identify its primary users.
2. Develop a framework identifying the full range of entities of interest to users and identifying the full range of relationships that exist between the entities.
3. Identify the functions the bibliographic record is supposed to perform for each entity.
4. Identify the key attributes of each entity or relationship that are needed to allow them to perform the functions mentioned in part 3.
5. Recommend a "basic level of functionality" that could be required of bibliographic records produced by national bibliographic agencies.[5]

The study group was appointed in 1991. By the time the report was completed, the group had thirteen commentators from nine countries as well as consultants. Drafts were completed over the next few years and discussed publicly at IFLA conferences in 1993 and 1994. A draft was submitted to international review in 1996, and the final draft, revised on the basis of comments received, was approved by the Section on Cataloguing in September 1997.

The objectives cited above imply that the model to be used for the study was "entity-relationship." Entity-relationship database modeling is discussed and explained in chapter 2 of this book. There were several models that could have been used for the study, but entity-relationship was chosen because it is a general model that can be used for any "domain" or "universe." As explained in 1994 by Barbara B. Tillett,

> The universe [for the model] is characterized in terms of the entities in it and the relationships that hold among them. As such, the conceptual schema is not restricted by the capabilities of any particular database system and is independent of any particular record definition. . . . It is perceived as being more easily understood, more stable, and easier to design than a schema conditioned by assumptions pertaining to what constitutes a bibliographic record or by storage and efficiency consideration.[6]

On this basis, FRBR is highly theoretical and, as mentioned above, meant to be system-neutral. Entity-relationship modeling was, however, developed in the computer science profession for a very practical purpose, to assist in the design of real databases, and so it seems logical that FRBR principles would work best when implemented in an entity-relationship database system. This book is written with that assumption in mind, and so when phrases like "FRBR record sets" are used, they are meant to evoke sets of records in an entity-relationship database. The entity-relationship model has great potential both to streamline data creation operations such as cataloging and, from the user's perspective, to allow much better search functionality and greater clarity in information display.

Entities are "key objects of interest to users" of a database (FRBR 3.1, p. 12). Accordingly, a bibliographic database would have different defined entities than a business or government database, since the users of the three types of databases would have different interests. Entities are discussed in this book in chapter 3. The relationships between these entities are discussed in chapter 4.

From the beginning, the FRBR study was intended to be centered on the needs of the user, and therefore it devotes a fair amount of space to discussion of users of bibliographic data, enumerating a list of four "user tasks" the study group decided were the basic things users needed to do when interacting with a bibliographic database:

- *Find* entities that correspond to the user's search criteria.
- *Identify* the entity (confirm that the entity found is the entity the user sought).
- *Select* an entity from the resulting group appropriate to the user's needs.
- *Obtain* the selected entity.

The user tasks are discussed in chapter 5 of this book.

Chapter 6 is a comparison of current cataloging practice with what could become the practice if FRBR principles are implemented.

Authority work and authority files were deliberately left out of FRBR (FRBR 1.3, p. 5). The study group did, however, recognize the need for analysis of authority data in the context of entities and relationships, in terms of user needs, and recommended this as an area for further study. Accordingly, IFLA appointed the Working Group on Functional Requirements and Numbering of Authority Records (FRANAR) within its Division of Bibliographic Control in 1998.[7] This working group had the following responsibilities:

- Define functional requirements of authority records, as an extension of the FRBR study.
- Study the feasibility, use, and possible structure of an International Standard Authority Data Number.
- Serve as the IFLA liaison to other groups with similar interests.

As with FRBR, the resulting study tried to be system- and rules-neutral. And like FRBR, it is also based on an entity-relationship model. The working group produced a draft for review in mid-2005. Taking numerous comments into account, it produced a second draft for comment in April 2007. Based on feedback received, a final draft will then be published.

The current draft, called Functional Requirements for Authority Data (FRAD), takes the same entities found in FRBR and extends them to the authority context.[8] FRAD also adds several entities not found in FRBR. The relationships between the entities it explores are also an extension of the relationships studied in FRBR. FRAD defines its users somewhat more narrowly than FRBR and has its own set of user tasks:

- *Find* entities that correspond to the user's search criteria.
- *Identify* the entity (confirm that the entity found is the entity the user sought).
- *Contextualize,* that is, place the entity into context.
- *Justify,* that is, document the data creator's reason for choosing the name on which a controlled access point is based.

The FRAD user tasks are discussed in chapter 5. The FRAD entities and relationships are discussed throughout chapters 3 and 4 of this book in the same context as their corresponding FRBR entities and relationships. The reader must bear in mind that this book's comments on and explanation of FRAD are based on the second draft, not the final publication. The final publication, which will likely be issued in 2008, will undoubtedly incorporate some changes from the 2007 draft.

The reader should also be aware of a third related working group, established by IFLA in 2005, dealing with Functional Requirements for Subject Authority Records (FRSAR). This group is to build on the model begun with FRBR and FRAD but concentrate on the entities that represent subjects. This group has not yet published a document.[9]

Finally, with respect both to FRBR and to FRAD, there is not yet any "official" body of literature or practical experience detailing how these documents should be interpreted. FRBR and FRAD concepts will be incorporated into RDA, the expected replacement for AACR2,[10] and are influential in the development of the new Statement of International Cataloguing Principles being developed by IFLA as a replacement for the Paris Principles.[11] But neither of these documents is yet published. Therefore, interpretations given in this book should be seen as only single possibilities among many but perhaps not the norm in the future.

Nevertheless, this volume provides a basic explanation of FRBR principles that will prepare the reader to follow the ongoing developments and understand their bearing on his or her day-to-day work.

NOTES

1. IFLA Study Group on the Functional Requirements for Bibliographic Records, *Functional Requirements for Bibliographic Records, Final Report,* UBCIM Publications, New Series, vol. 19 (München: K. G. Saur, 1998); also available at http://www.ifla.org/VII/s13/frbr/frbr.pdf or http://www.ifla.org/VII/s13/frbr/frbr.htm.
2. International Conference on Cataloguing Principles, *Report, International Conference on Cataloguing Principles, Paris, 9th–18th October 1961* (London: Organizing Committee of the International Conference on Cataloguing Principles, 1963).
3. For a list of currently published ISBDs, see http://www.ifla.org/VI/3/nd1/isbdlist.htm.
4. Much of the following is related in greater detail in Olivia M. A. Madison, "The Origins of the IFLA Study on Functional Requirements for Bibliographic Records," in *Functional Requirements for Bibliographic Records (FRBR): Hype or Cure-All?* edited by Patrick Le Boeuf (New York: Haworth Information Press, 2005), 15–37; also published as *Cataloging and Classification Quarterly* 39, nos. 3–4 (2005): 15–37.
5. The expectations ("terms of reference") of the study are quoted in full in Madison, "Origins," 35–37.
6. Barbara B. Tillett, "IFLA Study on the Functional Requirements of Bibliographic Records: Theoretical and Practical Foundations," speech delivered at the 1994 IFLA Conference held in Havana, Cuba, quoted in ibid., 29.
7. See Glenn E. Patton, "Extending FRBR to Authorities," in Le Boeuf, *Functional Requirements,* 39–48; also published as *Cataloging and Classification Quarterly* 39, nos. 3–4 (2005): 39–48. The working group's home page is http://www.ifla.org/VII/d4/wg-franar.htm.
8. IFLA Working Group on Functional Requirements and Numbering of Authority Records (FRANAR), *Functional Requirements for Authority Data: A Conceptual Model,* Draft 2007-04-01, available at http://www.ifla.org/VII/d4/FRANAR-ConceptualModel -2ndReview.pdf.
9. The group's home page is http://www.ifla.org/VII/s29/wgfrsar.htm.
10. *RDA: Resource Description and Access* is expected to be released in 2009. For more information, see http://www.collectionscanada.ca/jsc/rda.html.
11. Information about the development of the Statement of International Cataloguing Principles can be found in the IFLA Cataloguing Section's home page, http://www.ifla .org/VII/s13/index.htm. A report of the fourth meeting, held in Seoul, Korea, in August 2006, is found at http://www.nl.go.kr/icc/icc/main.php, together with the April 2007 draft of the statement.

2

The Entity-Relationship Model

According to its drafters, FRBR is based on the "entity-relationship analysis technique" (FRBR 2.3, p. 10). Entity-relationship is a database modeling technique introduced by Peter Chen in the mid-1970s.[1] Now widely used in database design, the model divides a given data universe (e.g., the data required to run a business) into specific entities linked by specific relationships.

An entity is something that can be distinctly identified.[2] For example, persons, corporate bodies, events, concepts, works, and publications may be entities. Entities are grouped into "entity sets." For example, the entity set *work* might contain many individual instances, such as James Joyce's *Ulysses,* Beethoven's Fifth Symphony, and the film *Gone with the Wind.* The entity set *person* might contain individual instances such as George Gershwin, Confucius, and Indira Gandhi. The entity set *event* might contain individual instances such as the eruption of Krakatoa in 1853, Hurricane Katrina (2005), and World War II.

Entity sets may have "subsets." For example, in the bibliographic universe the entity set *person* might have subsets such as "poet," "composer," and "editor." In a business environment this same entity set *person* might have the subsets "manager," "employee," "director," and the like. In a bibliographic database these business-related subsets are probably irrelevant, just as the bibliographic subsets would be irrelevant in a business database. The entity-relationship model is theoretical and does not specify the definition of the sets, which is left to the specific application.

In the model, individual entities can also have "roles." A role is the function an entity performs in a relationship.[3] In a bibliographic database, the subsets mentioned above ("poet," "composer," "editor") might better be considered roles than subsets of the entity set *person,* since a given person might perform any of those roles.

A relationship is an association among two or more entities. Chen gives as an example the relationship "father-son" between two person entities.[4] In the bibliographic universe, the relationship "adaptor-adaptation" might exist between an entity *person* and an entity *work*. An "earlier-later" relationship might exist between two *corporate body* entities. In the FRBR/FRAD model these relationships are usually expressed as actions, such as "produced by," "translated by," or "created by." Alternately, they may be expressed by phrases such as "has a subject" or "is part of."

As with entities, in the model, relationships are grouped in relationship sets. For example, in a given database the relationship set "adaptor-adaptation" might include many specific instances of this relationship. Theoretically the database design could include provision for queries retrieving all instances of a particular relationship set.

Entities and relationships are defined by attributes. Individual attributes or combinations of attributes are the characteristics that uniquely identify entities or relationships. For example, one attribute of the entity set *person* might be "name," because one of the characteristics of persons is that they have names. Another might be "dates" (e.g., birth and death dates). Attributes of the entities are clearly defined in FRBR chapter 4 and FRAD chapter 4. Attributes of relationships are a bit more difficult to conceptualize and in fact are not explicitly defined in FRBR or FRAD. Nevertheless, FRBR/FRAD relationships do potentially have attributes. For example, the "produced by" relationship might be thought to have the attribute of "date" (i.e., date of production) or "place" (where the entity was produced).

Entity-Relationship Diagramming

The entity-relationship model embodies a particular diagramming technique that is not used by FRBR or FRAD but is useful in explaining the model. I use this diagramming technique throughout this book in addition to FRBR/FRAD diagramming techniques because it portrays more graphically what a database based on the FRBR model might look like.

In entity-relationship diagramming, entities are drawn in rectangles, relationships in diamonds, and attributes in ovals. These are connected to each other by lines. (There are minor variants in entity-relationship diagramming, including various uses of arrows for connecting lines. Figure 2.1 shows one of the simpler types, without arrows, which is used in this book.) Each entity rectangle must be connected to other entity rectangles by relationship diamonds. Entity rectangles cannot be directly connected to each other. In entity-relationship diagramming, attribute ovals are connected only to single entity rectangles or relationship diamonds. They do not connect entities or relationships to each other.

A simplified entity-relationship diagram for the FRBR "produced by" relationship between the entity *manifestation* and the entity *person* or *corporate body* might look like figure 2.1. The figure shows that in a database founded on

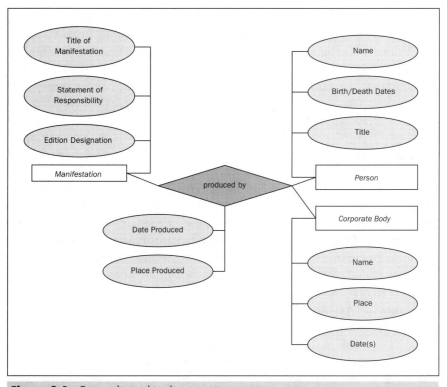

Figure 2.1 Entity-relationship diagramming

FRBR principles particular instances of the entity set *person* or *corporate body* might be related to instances of the entity set *manifestation* by a "produced by" relationship. The diagram shows that the entity *manifestation* has certain possible attributes, including "title of manifestation," "statement of responsibility," and "edition designation" (see chapter 3 for details on attributes of entities). In individual instances of *manifestation,* values would be provided for each of these attributes, such as "Syrinx" for the attribute "title of manifestation," "by Claude Debussy" for the attribute "statement of responsibility," or "new and revised edition" for the attribute "edition designation." In this book's illustrations, attribute values are recorded after the name of the attribute and a colon. In this book I refer to "FRBR record sets." These are sets of records for individual instances of entities linked to each other by relationships. Within each entity record, values for the attributes associated with the instance of the entity are recorded.

The diagram in figure 2.1 is based on FRBR, although greatly simplified. This diagram also departs from FRBR in assigning "date produced" and "place produced" as attributes of the "produced by" relationship set rather than of the *manifestation* entity set (see FRBR 4.4.4 and 4.4.6, pp. 42–43). As noted above, FRBR does not assign attributes to relationships, but the entity-relationship model does. The FRBR model could thus be described as being based on entity-relationship theory but not following the classical expression of that theory in all respects.

FRBR Diagramming

FRBR has two diagramming styles, one for entity-relationship sets and another for specific instances of entity-relationship. FRBR diagramming for entity-relationship sets might be described as a simplified version of the entity-relationship diagramming shown above, in which the entities are drawn in rectangles but the relationships are simply represented by lines connecting the rectangles, with the nature of the relationship shown by words next to the lines. Attributes are not shown at all in these diagrams.

Figure 2.2 reproduces FRBR figure 3.1 (p. 13). *Work, expression, manifestation,* and *item* are entities; "is realized through," "is embodied in," and "is exemplified by" are relationships. Single arrows mean that only one instance of an entity can occur in the relationship; double arrows mean that more than one instance can occur. For example, according to the model, more than one instance of the entity *item* can occur in relation to a manifestation, but only one manifestation can occur in relation to an item. To put it another way, a manifestation can have many items, but an item can stem from only one manifestation (see detailed discussion of these entities in chapter 3).

The entity-relationship diagram shown in figure 2.1 is based on part of FRBR figure 3.2 (p. 14). In FRBR diagramming the same relationship, between the entity *manifestation* and the entities *person* or *corporate body,* would be diagrammed as in figure 2.3.

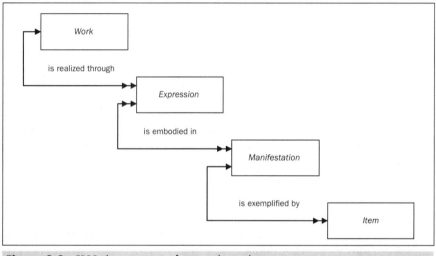

Figure 2.2 FRBR diagramming of entity-relationship sets

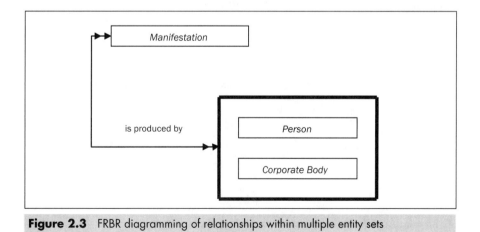

Figure 2.3 FRBR diagramming of relationships within multiple entity sets

The bold box around *person* and *corporate body* is a kind of shorthand that means that the relationship can apply to either of the entities. In FRAD this same information is conveyed by a dashed rectangle surrounding the entities. In this book I use both diagramming styles, depending on whether I am illustrating FRBR or FRAD.

Figures 2.2 and 2.3 show the FRBR diagramming used to show entity sets. When FRBR diagrams particular instances of an entity, it uses a different style, as seen in figure 2.4. This "outline" diagramming shows a relationship between *manifestation* and *corporate body*, the same relationship shown in figure 2.3, but with specific instances of the entities *corporate body* (**cb**) and *manifestation* (**m**). The type of relationship between the entities in this case is not made explicit; the indentation shows only that a relationship exists. In figure 2.4 the three manifestations (**m₁** to **m₃**) are shown by their secondary position to have some relationship to a particular corporate body.

If necessary, such FRBR outline diagramming can be used to show explicitly the relationship between instances of entities, using an arrow notation around the relationship expressed as a phrase. The "produced by" relationship between a manifestation and a corporate body might be shown as in figure 2.5. In FRBR diagramming, the arrow points away from the entity that is the subject of the phrase. For instance, the arrow following "is the producer of" points away from Kelmscott Press, and thus the diagram could be read in standard English as "Kelmscott Press is the producer of the 1891 publication of *Poems by the Way* by William Morris, the 1892 publication of *The Recuyell of the Historyes of Troye* by Raoul Lefevre, and the 1896 publication of *The Works of Geoffrey Chaucer*." Conversely it could be read "The 1891 publication of *Poems by the Way* by William Morris has a producer, Kelmscott Press."

- **cb₁**   Kelmscott Press
    - **m₁**   the 1891 publication of *Poems by the Way* by William Morris
    - **m₂**   the 1892 publication of *The Recuyell of the Historyes of Troye* by Raoul Lefevre
    - **m₃**   the 1896 publication of *The Works of Geoffrey Chaucer*
    - ...

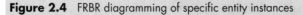

Figure 2.4   FRBR diagramming of specific entity instances

- **cb**$_1$ Kelmscott Press

  is the producer of →

  ← has a producer

  - **m**$_1$ the 1891 publication of *Poems by the Way* by William Morris

  - **m**$_2$ the 1892 publication of *The Recuyell of the Historyes of Troye* by Raoul Lefevre

  - **m**$_3$ the 1896 publication of *The Works of Geoffrey Chaucer*

  - ...

Figure 2.5 FRBR diagramming of specific relationship instances

NOTES

1. Peter Pin-Shan Chen, "The Entity-Relationship Model: Toward a Unified View of Data," *ACM Transactions on Database Systems* 1, no. 1 (1976): 9–36. See also P. Chen, "Entity-Relationship Modeling: Historical Events, Future Trends, and Lessons Learned," in *Software Pioneers: Contributions to Software Engineering,* edited by Manfred Broy and Ernst Denert (Berlin: Springer, 2002), 100–114. PDF file of paper available at http://bit.csc.lsu.edu/~chen/pdf/Chen_Pioneers.pdf. For a detailed examination of entity-relationship, see Bernhard Thalheim, *Entity-Relationship Modeling: Foundations of Database Technology* (Berlin: Springer, 2000).
2. Chen, "Entity-Relationship Model," 10.
3. Ibid., 12.
4. Ibid., 10.

The FRBR Entities

The FRBR Groups

FRBR chapter 3 defines the entities used in the model. They are logically arranged in three groups. Group 1 entities are "the products of intellectual or artistic endeavour": *work, expression, manifestation,* and *item.* Group 1 entities have traditionally been the focus of library catalog records.

Group 2 comprises the entities responsible for the production of Group 1 entities or those that own Group 1 entities: *person, corporate body,* and an entity defined for FRAD, *family* (FRAD 3.4, p. 8). The word "production" is used in this book in its usual English-language sense. For example, a poet can "produce" a poem (work); a translator can "produce" a translation (expression); an illustrator can "produce" illustrations for an illustrated text (expression); a publisher can "produce" a publication (manifestation); a binder can "produce" the binding on an individual book, a part of a FRBR item.

"Produce" also has a specific meaning for FRBR, as the name of the relationship between a Group 2 entity and a manifestation (see figure 2.3).

The model as it currently stands does not take into account certain other relationships aside from production or ownership that persons, corporate bodies, or families might have with Group 1 entities. For example, the addressee of a collection of letters has no production or ownership relationship with any Group 1 entity, but in our bibliographic tradition it is thought useful to bring out this relationship in our databases. Similarly in rare materials cataloging traditions it is common to bring out the relationship between a signer (a person, a Group 2 entity) and the printed book he or she signed (an item, a Group 1 entity), even though no ownership or production relationship might exist.

Group 3 comprises entities that "serve as the subjects of *works*" (FRBR 3.1.3, p. 16). Note that Group 1 and Group 2 entities can also "serve as the subjects of *works*." In addition, Group 3 defines four additional entities: *concept, object, event,* and *place.*

Limiting the relationship of these entities to a single Group 1 entity, *work,* seems unnecessarily confining, since Group 1, 2, and 3 entities in some instances can also "serve as subjects" of other Group 1 entities. For example, the text of a famous literary work is sometimes published with extensive introduction and notes. Such an edition might have significant biographical information about the author or extensive criticism of the work, enough to warrant a subject heading. A well-known example of this is *The Annotated Alice* (New York: Norton, 2000). Its record might appropriately contain the subject "Carroll, Lewis, 1832–1898— Criticism and interpretation." This concept has no relationship to the work entity, but rather to this expression. Although probably most subject relationships would be at the work level, by no means all are, and it might be preferable in FRBR simply to define Group 3 entities as "entities that serve as subjects of Group 1 entities."

Additionally, as currently written, FRBR does not deal well with genre/form relationships with Group 1 entities. One of Cutter's objectives of the catalog was to "show the user what the library has . . . in a given kind of literature."[1] This has become a common relationship brought out in current library catalogs. Although, for example, "English poetry" is a concept in FRBR, when used to bring out the genre of a work it does not serve as a subject of the work. Gray's "Elegy Written in a Country Churchyard" is not *about* English poetry, it is *an example of* English poetry. The relationship between the poem and the concept "English poetry" is not an "about" relationship but an "is" relationship. It appears that for the moment this common relationship must be subsumed under the Group 3 entity *concept,* but it does not fit well. This could be solved by broadening slightly the definition of Group 3 to include entities that "serve as subjects, genres, or forms" of a Group 1 entity and adding another entity, *form.* Note that "form" is defined as an attribute of *work* (see discussion below). It would probably be better to consider it as an entity with a relationship with the FRBR Group 1 entities rather than as an attribute of one of them.

Work

Work is defined in FRBR as "a distinct intellectual or artistic creation," expanded in FRAD to specify that this refers to the intellectual or artistic *content* (FRBR 3.2.1, p. 16; FRAD 3.4, p. 9). This is a beguilingly simple definition, but in fact what constitutes a work is a complex question and has been discussed for years.[2] One thing is clear, though: the entity *work* represents an abstract concept. The theme from the Debussy flute composition *Syrinx* may pass through my head, or I may even hum or sing the notes, but that event is not the work. I might play the entire piece, but that event is not the work. I might even write it down in musical notation—still not the work! All three of these events have some relationship to the work, as do the performances of other flutists and the various printed versions of the piece—or indeed, Debussy's original manuscript. But they are not themselves the work in the abstract FRBR sense. The work is recognizable because we have all those performances and publications. If anything, it is what all those performances and publications have in common. To paraphrase FRBR, when we speak of *Syrinx* as a work, we are not thinking of a particular performance or publication of the work but of the intellectual creation that lies behind the various expressions of the work. In the words of Richard Smiraglia, for FRBR, the *work* is a "set of impressions (ideational concepts) in the mind of its creator . . . [the] 'authorial intention.' Once the creator has mulled over these impressions sufficiently to formulate an ordered presentation, then they may take on the characteristics of expression" (on *expression,* see below).[3]

Still, in common speech we do behave as though *work* were more concrete. We have the feeling that Zukerman's performance of *Syrinx* and Galway's are "the same work," even though they might have been performed in radically different ways. We think of various printed editions as the same work even though their editors might have introduced completely different notes, dynamic levels, and speed designations. We accept that these are all the same work, even though there might be minor differences between them. Indeed, there is a huge difference between a performance of *Syrinx* (an aural experience) and the printed notes of *Syrinx* on a few sheets of paper, and yet we seem to accept these as the same thing, the same work.

Yet at some point differences become important. If I took the same notes and played them backward, would they remain the same work or would they be a new work? What if I played them on the clarinet instead of the flute? Suppose a composer takes the original unaccompanied tune and turns it into a piece for marching band? What if the notes remain the same but the rhythm changes, as in a jazz version? What if the composer simply takes the tune or parts of the tune and quotes it in a new piece? Is the new piece the same work? Most people would agree that at some point a line is crossed and a new work is created; it is no longer the same work. But where is that line?

FRBR points out that this is a cultural question: "The line of demarcation . . . between one *work* and another may in fact be viewed differently from one culture to another. Consequently the bibliographic conventions established by various cultures or national groups may differ in terms of the criteria they use for determining the boundaries between one *work* and another." Views probably also differ within cultures, even between individuals.

Given that FRBR emphasizes the fluidity of the concept behind the entity *work,* it is somewhat surprising that the document immediately gets down to the business of defining exactly where that line or boundary is (FRBR 3.2.1, pp. 16–17). In FRBR, variants that incorporate revisions or updates to an existing work are regarded as the same work, as are abridgments, enlargements, the addition of accompaniment to a musical work, and translations from one language to another. The line is crossed to "new work" with "paraphrases, rewritings, adaptations for children, parodies, musical variations on a theme, and free transcriptions of a musical composition," as well as "adaptations of a *work* from one literary form or art form to another" and "abstracts, digests, and summaries."

The line between works in FRBR appears to be based on one specific cultural tradition, namely the Anglo-American tradition embodied in AACR2. FRBR's same work/different work listings are quite close to AACR2's, as can be seen from the following enumeration:

Same Work in AACR2

- Unchanged texts with illustrations added (21.11A)
- Revisions of texts for which the original author is considered responsible (21.12)
- Abridgments, if extensive rewriting is not involved (21.12)
- Texts published with commentary if the original text is emphasized (21.13C)
- Translations (21.14)
- Texts published with biographical or critical work, if the chief source emphasizes the text (21.15A)
- Reproductions of artworks (photographic or in the same medium as the original) (21.16B)
- Arrangements of musical works (21.18B)

- Musical works with text, accompaniment, or additional parts added (21.19A, 21.21)
- Recordings of musical works (21.13)

Different Work in AACR2

- Paraphrases, rewritings, adaptations for children, adaptations that produce versions in different literary forms (21.10)
- Illustrations for a text published separately from the text (22.11B)
- Revisions of texts for which the original author is no longer considered responsible (21.12B)
- Abridgments if extensive rewriting is involved (21.12 and 21.10)
- Texts published with commentary if the commentary is emphasized (21.13B)
- Texts published with biographical or critical work, if the chief source emphasizes the biographical or critical work (21.15A)
- Texts that have been set to music (21.19A)
- Filmed versions of literary works (21.6)
- An artwork produced in a different medium from the original (21.16A)
- Free transcriptions of musical works, variations on a musical theme, or paraphrases in the general style of another musical work (21.18C)

In FRBR, if two versions are considered the same work, they are called different expressions of the work. If they are not, they are called separate works. Given these boundaries, the various putative versions of *Syrinx* above might be diagrammed as in figure 3.1.

Attributes of Work

As with all entities in the entity-relationship model, *work* is defined by a set of attributes that distinguishes it from other entities in the FRBR model, and differences between the values in the attributes distinguish between different instances of the entity *work.* Twelve attributes have been defined for *work,* not all of which are relevant to every instance of a work (FRBR 4.2, pp. 32–35).

The first, and perhaps most important, attribute of *work* is "title of the work" (FRBR 4.2.1, p. 33). As an identifying characteristic of a work, in the Anglo-American tradition, "title" may equate to "uniform title." FRBR defines it as "the

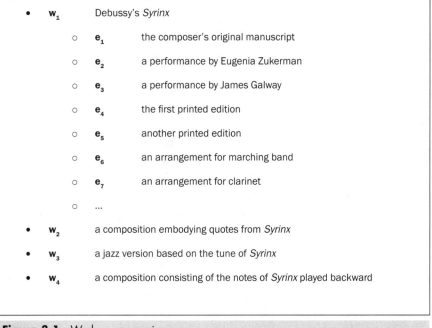

- **w₁**   Debussy's *Syrinx*
    - ○ **e₁**   the composer's original manuscript
    - ○ **e₂**   a performance by Eugenia Zukerman
    - ○ **e₃**   a performance by James Galway
    - ○ **e₄**   the first printed edition
    - ○ **e₅**   another printed edition
    - ○ **e₆**   an arrangement for marching band
    - ○ **e₇**   an arrangement for clarinet
    - ○ ...
- **w₂**   a composition embodying quotes from *Syrinx*
- **w₃**   a jazz version based on the tune of *Syrinx*
- **w₄**   a composition consisting of the notes of *Syrinx* played backward

Figure 3.1   Work vs. expression

word, phrase, or group of characters naming the *work*." When there is more than one title associated with the work, one is normally chosen as the principal title used to identify the work. In the case of *Syrinx*, the "title of the work" attribute is "Debussy, Claude, 1862–1918. Syrinx." When he originally composed the piece, Debussy gave *Syrinx* a different title, "Flûte de Pan." FRBR acknowledges that works often have more than one title associated with them and suggests that they normally be treated as variants. In an authority system this would be accomplished by a system of cross-references; thus in the MARC authority format the title "Debussy, Claude, 1862–1918. Flûte de Pan" would be coded as a variant form in a 400 field. In a FRBR entity-relationship database, this variant title would be recorded in the work-level record, and indeed in such a record it might not be necessary to choose one authoritative form.

The FRAD model does not include "title" as an attribute of *work*. This is because FRAD treats the "name" (i.e., title) of a work as a separate entity within the model. The entity *name* is linked to the entity *work* in FRAD through a "known by" relationship, that is, a work is "known by" a name. The FRAD entity *name* has several attributes, including "type of name," defined as the category of the name, for example, personal name or corporate name. In the case of the name of a work, the type of name would be "title of work."

This departure from the FRBR model might seem overly complex, but it is necessary for the FRAD model because it clarifies the relationships between several FRAD entities. Within FRAD, a bibliographic entity such as a work, person, or object is "known by" a name; in turn, the name is the "basis for" a controlled access point, itself a FRAD entity. In turn, a controlled access point may be "registered in" an authority record, another entity (see figure 3.2, based on FRAD figure 2, p. 7, and figure 5, p. 63). For further discussion of the need for the entity *name* in FRAD, see FRAD 3.1, p. 3, and FRAD 4, p. 16.

How this attribute might play out in a FRBR record set for *Syrinx* is illustrated in figures 3.3a and 3.3b. These figures are given in entity-relationship diagramming style, as described in chapter 2. In a database founded on FRBR principles, each entity (rectangle) would have its own record. It would be linked with other entities by one or more relationships (diamond). Values for attributes (oval) would be recorded as part of the appropriate entity record. Figure 3.3a diagrams the record set according to the FRBR model, that is, considering "title of the work" to be an attribute of the entity *work*. Figure 3.3b diagrams the set according to the FRAD model, where the title of the work is a separate entity, *name*. Other similar diagrams in this book follow the FRAD model.

A second attribute of *work* is "form of work" (FRBR 4.2.2, p. 33; FRAD 4.4, p. 19), "the class to which the *work* belongs." The form of *Syrinx*, using current

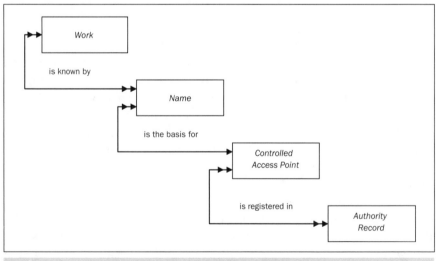

Figure 3.2 Relationship of work to other FRAD entities

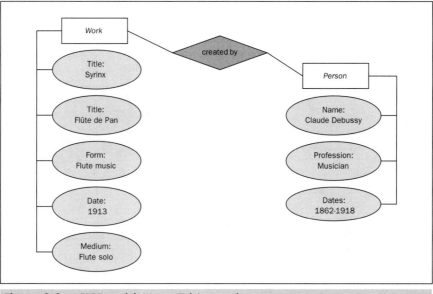

Figure 3.3a FRBR model: Name (Title) as attribute

LCSH form terms, would be "flute music" (see figure 3.3b). But note that a given work could have more than one form, since there is often overlap between forms. For example, a short science fiction work would have at least two values for this attribute, "science fiction" and "short stories."

A problem with using "form" as an attribute of *work* is that "form" might itself better be considered an entity, either a separately defined entity or a subclass of the entity *concept* (discussed below). "Science fiction" is a form term when used to describe what a work *is,* but it can also be used as a concept term when used to describe what a work is *about.* In either case it is an entity in itself and as such should not be considered an attribute of another entity. Instead, in an entity-relationship database it has a relationship to the other entity (e.g., to a work). See figure 3.4 for a diagram of *Syrinx* using a model in which form is an entity related to the work rather than an attribute of the work.

A second problem with "form" as an attribute of *work* is that as an entity *form* can have relationships with the other FRBR Group 1 entities as well. For example, "translations" (or "translations into English") is a form, but it would be applicable only at the expression level, not the work level. If we leave the realm of literary form terms, many form terms have application only at the manifestation level, such as "limited editions." Some form terms are even applicable at the item

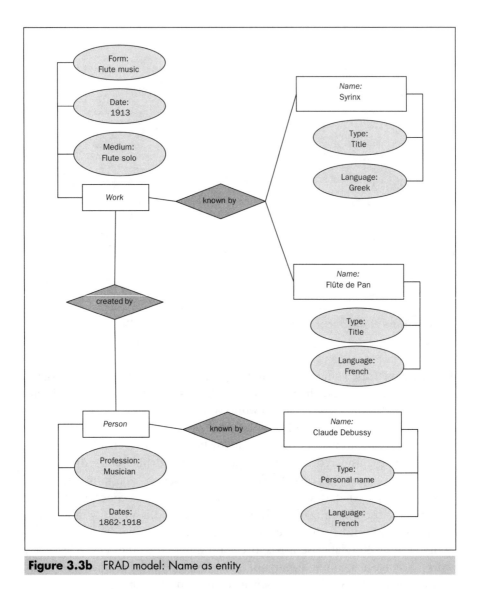

Figure 3.3b FRAD model: Name as entity

level, such as terms describing the unique bindings of early printed books (e.g., "calf bindings"), where each item has a different binding because the practice during the period was for the bookseller to sell sheets to the book buyer, who then took them to a binder to have them bound.

"Date of the work" is another attribute of *work* (FRBR 4.2.3, p. 33; FRAD 4.4, p. 19). This is the date the work was originally created (FRAD has modified this to "the first date . . . associated with the work"). Although *Syrinx* was not

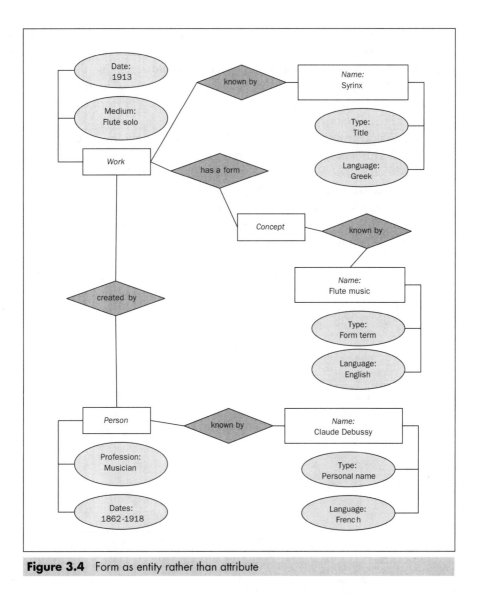

Figure 3.4 Form as entity rather than attribute

published until 1927, it was originally composed in 1913, so the latter date would be recorded in the work-level record for *Syrinx* (see figure 3.3b).

There are two problems with date as attribute of the entity *work,* one theoretical and the other practical. First, the date attribute is associated with an event, the creation of the work. In the entity-relationship model, this event is associated with a relationship, the "created by" relationship with the entities *person, corporate body,* or *family* (see discussion of this relationship in chapter 4, pp. 106–7). As noted in chapter 2, relationships also have attributes in the entity-relationship model, but these are not defined in the FRBR model. Assuming attributes of relationships should be defined, it would seem that the "date of the work" attribute would better be assigned to the relationship, that is, when the "created by" relationship took place, rather than to the work entity. For a diagram using this model, see figure 3.5.

The practical problem consists in the difficulty in pinpointing the date a work was created. This is easy enough in the case of *Syrinx,* which is well documented in sources such as *The New Grove Dictionary of Music and Musicians.* But most works are not like *Syrinx,* and an expectation to record the date a work was created in an entity record for the work might not be realistic. A fallback might be to assume that the date of first publication is the date of the work, but such a practical solution is not congruent with the reality of how works are created.

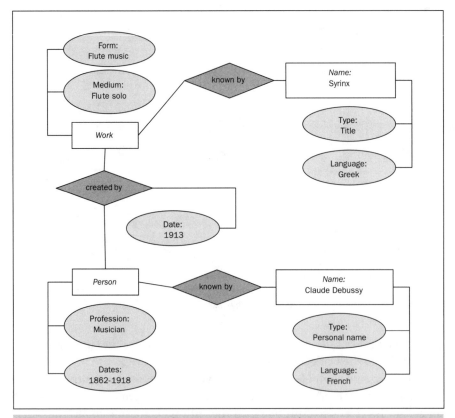

Figure 3.5 Date as attribute of relationship rather than of entity

This book carries a publication date of 2008, but its manuscript was developed over two or three years. Is the date of the work the year the final manuscript was handed over to the publisher? In the case of this book, since it was published early in 2008, it is a reasonable assumption that the manuscript was completed in 2007. But what about a book published later in the year? Using the above criterion, the work might have been "created" the same year as its publication. Clearly, pinning down "date of the work" will be difficult. Is it reasonable to expect the creator of a database to discover the date the work was created in order to create an entity record for the work? Such details need to be worked out before we can truly move to a FRBR model.

FRBR recognizes that different works sometimes share a title, so a fourth attribute of the entity *work* is "other distinguishing characteristic," defined as "any characteristic that serves to differentiate the *work* from another *work* with the same title" (FRBR 4.2.4, p. 33; FRAD 4.4, p. 21). When using the Anglo-American system of uniform titles, this most commonly happens for works of unknown or diffuse authorship, where the uniform title would consist of a title alone, not a name-title combination (as with *Syrinx*). For example, there are several works sharing the title "Mother Goose," including the collection of nursery rhymes and several choreographic works. One of the choreographic works might be distinguished from the collection of rhymes by (1) the fact that it is a choreographic work and (2) by the name of its principal choreographer. In the current environment this is accomplished by adding a parenthetical qualifier to the base title, such as "Mother Goose (Choreographic work : Staats)." In a FRBR work record, this might instead be accomplished by the inclusion in the record of the choreographer's name. More likely, the form entity associated with the work record (choreographic work) and date attribute (1915 in this case) in the work record itself would be enough to distinguish between these works in the FRBR environment. The entity record for the choreographer Leo Staats would also be linked to the work record showing his relationship to the work.

Other attributes of *work* are "intended termination" (i.e., whether it is intended to have a termination, not the date of its intended termination—this attribute has continuing resources in mind) (FRBR 4.2.5, p. 34), "intended audience" (FRBR 4.2.6, p. 34), and "context for the work" (FRBR 4.2.7, p. 34). Three attributes have been defined for musical works, "medium of performance," "numeric designation," and "key" (FRBR 4.2.8–10, p. 34), and two for cartographic works, "coordinates" and "equinox" (FRBR 4.2.11–12, pp. 34–35).

FRAD adds four further attributes (FRAD 4.4, p. 20): "subject of the work," subject aspects of the work and its content; "place of origin of the work," the country or other area from which the work originated; "original language of the work," the language in which the work was first expressed; and "history," information pertaining to the history of the work.

"Original language" and "history" seem reasonable and appropriate as attributes of *work*. "Language of expression" is an attribute of the entity *expression*, but it does seem useful to record the language of the first expression as an attribute of the work, at least in the case of text-based works. However, the first two FRAD attributes, "subject" and "place," might better be considered separate entities with a relationship to the work, especially since they are elsewhere defined as entities both in FRBR and in FRAD. Any of the entities can have a subject relationship with a work (FRBR figure 3.3, p. 15; FRBR 3.1.3, p. 16), and *place* is a specific Group 3 entity (FRBR 3.2.10, p. 27; FRAD 3.4, p. 12).

As applicable, values for all these attributes would be embedded in the work record in a FRBR entity-relationship database. Ideally the values would be searchable and would allow for collocation (e.g., the user should be able to find all works with the same "date of work" attribute). One of the advantages of a FRBR database is that these values would need to be recorded only once for any given work instead of every time a new edition or version is recorded. Under current cataloging practices, for example, every time a new copy of the printed music for *Syrinx* or a new recorded performance of the work is added to a library's catalog, the uniform title and form of the work are repeated in separate records. In the case of *Syrinx* this is a minor nuisance, but in the case of works that have been published hundreds of times, the savings of having to record work attributes only once, in a work record, instead of repeating them in separate records for each publication would be significant.

Superworks

There has been some discussion of the need for a FRBR Group 1 entity at a higher level than *work*. In figure 3.1, the expressions e_1 to e_7 are grouped in a set by their relationship to w_1, the work Debussy's *Syrinx*. It has been argued that a similar set grouping of the four related works diagrammed in figure 3.1 would be useful, by means of a higher-level entity that might be called a *superwork*.[4] The purpose of such an entity would be to allow better collocation between related works in catalogs and databases.

Expression

The concept of *work*, although complex, has been around a long time, and most people seem to have an intuitive grasp of its meaning. Not so with the concept of *expression,* an entity introduced in FRBR that has caused a fair amount of confusion.

Expression is defined as "the intellectual or artistic realization of a *work* in the form of alpha-numeric, musical, or choreographic notation, sound, image, object, movement, etc., or any combination of such forms" (FRBR 3.2.2, p. 18; FRAD 3.4, p. 9). In FRBR, a work is said to be "realized" through its expression (see FRBR figure 3.1, p. 13). What does "realization" mean here? In its pure etymological sense, it means to make something real. This implies that a work is not real until it finds an expression.

Integral to the concept of *expression* in FRBR is the concept of *form.* For a work to be realized it has to take some form. For example, the first form a text-based work takes is usually a set of written words. In an oral society, this first form might instead be a spoken recitation of the words. Either of these would be the first expression of the work. Similarly, the first form a musical work takes could be a performance, or it could be notated music. Either of these would be the first expression of the work.

Form is important to the definition of *expression* only in its most general sense. FRBR explicitly defines the boundaries of *expression* as excluding aspects of physical form such as layout, script, and the like, so long as these are not integral to the work. Thus several copies of an author's manuscript might constitute the same expression, even though she printed them out using various fonts, type sizes, margin settings, or line spacings, so long as changes to the text were not made between printouts. Indeed, the author's manuscript of a work might well be considered the same expression as the first printed publication, so long as the intellectual content remains the same. On the other hand, in the case of a calligraphic rendition of a verse from the Koran, layout and script would probably be considered integral to the (art) work, and thus in this case changes would create a new expression, if not a new work.

FRBR as originally written holds that *any* change to the work, however minor, creates a new expression, so the original manuscript would be the same expression as the printed publication only if no changes were made when the manuscript was printed, an unlikely though possible occurrence. In a change to the text of FRBR proposed in late 2006, this rather severe interpretation of *expression* is softened somewhat, removing the language stating that any change, no matter how minor, constitutes a new expression. The new wording retains the basic idea but allows for minor variants within an expression: "If a text is revised or modified, the resulting *expression* is considered to be a new *expression.* Minor changes, such as corrections of spelling and punctuation, etc., are normally considered as variations within the same *expression.*"[5] This change is sensible.

The original strict interpretation implied a requirement that catalogers compare versions to detect differences, "no matter how minor."

Application of this sensible change will certainly require judgment. Does the phrase "corrections of spelling and punctuation" extend to national differences as between U.K. and U.S. releases of the same novel, with British spelling and punctuation conventions in one and American English in the other? Or is this limited to corrections of misspelled words? What about a version of a sixteenth-century text that has modernized the spelling conventions but otherwise left the wording untouched? Are these the same expression? So far the authors of FRBR have sensibly left this to the cataloger's judgment, and the decision may depend on the needs of the application. The proposed change leaves the door open for this, noting that some applications of the model, such as a rare book catalog, might take a very strict view of what constitutes a new expression, because rare book libraries need to distinguish between versions of a publication based on variants other entities might consider minor. Other entities remain free to consider these the same expression while the rare book library is free to consider them different expressions.

By definition, the basic form a work is realized in is one distinguishing factor between expressions. A performance of *Syrinx* is a different expression from a version realized through musical notation, though both are the same work (see w_1 of figure 3.1). A manuscript of a poem in electronic text format is a different expression from an oral rendition of the poem. These are two different ways the work might be realized.

Like *work*, *expression* is abstract. One cannot point to a physical object and say that that is the expression of a given work. In the situation described above where an author prints out several copies of a manuscript, all with different type sizes, spacing, and so forth, what these printouts have in common, that is, the text itself realized in an ink on paper form, might be said to come close to the idea of *expression*.

Attributes of Expression

Expression has been assigned twenty-five attributes in FRBR, most of which will not be applicable to any given expression. Additionally, a given expression inherits all of the attributes of its work.

As with *work*, the first attribute of *expression* is "title of the expression" (FRBR 4.3.1, p. 36). Although FRBR states that there may be more than one title associated with an expression, it would seem that, as an identifying characteristic of *expression*, "title of the expression" in the Anglo-American cataloging tradition would need to be "uniform title," with other titles associated with the expression considered variants. Although catalogers commonly think of uniform titles as applying to works, most actually apply to expressions. For example, the uniform title for the *Odyssey* in its original language, Greek (the first expression of the work), is

> Homer. Odyssey

If translated into English (another expression), its uniform title becomes

> Homer. Odyssey. English

These are expression-level uniform titles. Note that in both of these cases the AACR2 uniform title is not designed to distinguish between expressions within a single language. For instance, the *Odyssey* has been translated into English many times. Since the intellectual content differs between these translations, each is a separate expression. Similarly, various editions of the original Greek text of the *Odyssey* may differ in content, depending on the editor's interpretation of the manuscript evidence. These, too, are separate expressions. In neither case does current cataloging practice distinguish between them. Pope's translation of the *Odyssey* will be assigned the same uniform title as Knox's. FRAD (3.4, p. 10) points out that uniform title–controlled access points in current practice normally serve to collocate related expressions rather than differentiating between individual expressions.

Note that we commonly think that the uniform title "Homer. Odyssey" applies to the work. In fact, it applies to the Greek-language expressions of the *Odyssey*. As procedures are worked out to move to a FRBR environment, this discrepancy will need to be resolved, assuming uniform titles continue to be used to identify works and expressions. One resolution could be an agreement to use the same identifier for a work and its first expression.

One case in current cataloging practice where expression-level uniform titles come close to distinguishing between all expressions is Bible uniform titles. These uniform titles contain a section for the work (e.g., Bible. O.T. Joshua), then the language of the expression (e.g., English), then the name of the version, a concept close to the FRBR *expression* (e.g., New American):

> Bible. O.T. Joshua. English. New American ...

Bible uniform titles do not distinguish between various editions of a given version, which would be separate expressions (the date element in Bible uniform titles is a manifestation-related element), but they still come closer to identifying the FRBR expression entity than other AACR2 uniform titles (on Bible uniform titles, see AACR2 25.17–18).

"Title of the expression" is not an attribute of *expression* in FRAD. As discussed above under the attribute "title of the work" (pp. 19–20), FRAD considers the title of the expression to be a separate entity, called *name.*

A second attribute of *expression* is "form of expression" (FRBR 4.3.2, p. 36; FRAD 4.5, p. 21). As noted above, form is an important attribute used to distinguish between otherwise identical expressions. Form is "the means by which a *work* is realized." This can include concepts such as alpha-numeric notation (i.e., text), musical notation, sound, and dance. The form of the first expression of the *Odyssey* was spoken word, since it was composed before writing came into general use among the Greeks. The form of the first expression of the New American version of the book of Joshua was alpha-numeric notation. The value for this attribute ("form of expression") would be recorded in an expression-level record in a FRBR database and might in combination with an expression identifier such as a uniform title be used to distinguish it from other similar expression-level records. See figure 3.6 for an example diagramming a Spanish-language oral expression of the *Odyssey*, with the "form of expression" attribute "spoken word."

The attribute "date of expression" is the date when the expression was first created (FRBR 4.3.3, p. 36; FRAD 4.5, p. 21). See, for example, figure 3.6, where the value for "date of expression" is "2003." In the case of the first expression of a work, "date of expression" would likely be the same date as the date of creation of the work. In the case of *Syrinx*, the value for the "date of the work" attribute is "1913" (see figure 3.3b). This is also the year Debussy first realized the work in musical notation (first expression), so this would also be the value for "date of expression" in the expression-level record. If the first publication of *Syrinx* (1927) contained identical content to the 1913 manuscript, it would be a second instance of the first expression of the work (see figure 3.7). Each instance is called *manifestation* (see below). The expression-level record would have "1913" for the "date of expression" even though the publication of the second manifestation took place in 1927. In figure 3.7, note that the date of the work, the date of the expression, and the date of the first manifestation are all "1913."

The same two objections apply to "date of expression" as an attribute of the entity *expression* as to "date of the work" as an attribute of the entity *work* (see pp. 23–25). First, the date is associated with an event, realization, which is expressed in FRBR as a relationship, not an entity, so the "date" attribute would probably better be applied to the relationship rather than to the entity. Second, there are very real practical problems in determining the value of "date of expression" in order to complete an expression-level record in a FRBR database. Except in well-known cases such as *Syrinx*, the date of the expression will be unknown to the

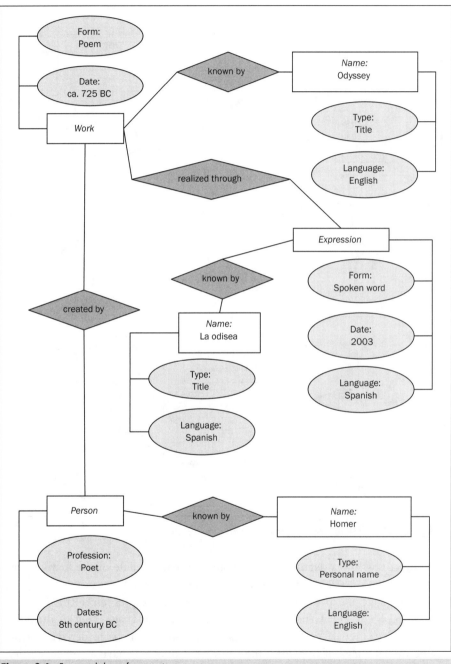

Figure 3.6 Form and date of expression

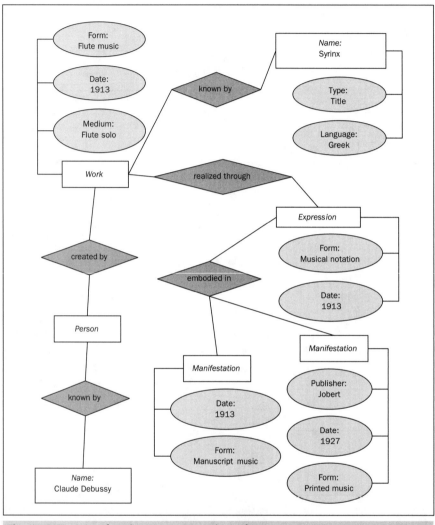

Figure 3.7 Date of work, expression, and manifestation

cataloger. Possibly a default position could be that the date of the first known manifestation is to be recorded as the "date of expression."

"Language of expression" is the fourth attribute of *expression* (FRBR 4.3.4, p. 36; FRAD 4.5, p. 21). To be noted here is the fact that language is *not* an attribute of *work*. The language of the first expression of a work is not considered in FRBR to be the language of the work; the work itself does not have a language (see, however, FRAD 4.4, p. 20, where "original language of the work" is proposed as a new attribute of *work*). On the other hand, language is one of the attributes that may be used to distinguish one expression from another, although it must be used in combination with other attributes since more than one expression of a work can exist in a single language.

Another point that will need to be worked out as FRBR is implemented is how broadly "language of expression" is to be interpreted. Does "language" include musical or mathematical notation? If not, "language of expression" would be inapplicable as an attribute for musical and purely mathematical works. And could it somehow apply to works in the visual arts, such as sculpture?

The attribute "other distinguishing characteristic" (FRBR 4.3.5, p. 36; FRAD 4.5, p. 21) would come into play if distinct expressions had the same title, form, date, and language and needed to be distinguished in some other way. In current cataloging practices this attribute corresponds to such things as edition statements and version names (as seen above with Bible uniform titles).

Another attribute that could distinguish one expression from another is "extent of expression" (FRBR 4.3.8, p. 37). This attribute is a concrete measurement of the otherwise rather abstract concept of *expression*. Examples might be "the exact number of words (letters, etc.) in Pope's English-language expression of the *Odyssey*" or "the exact running time of Eugenia Zukerman's performance (expression) of *Syrinx*." This attribute has great potential for computer-assisted distinctions between expressions.

The six attributes just reviewed appear to be the principal attributes that could be used to distinguish between different expressions of a single work. Many of the others are distinguishing attributes as well, but they apply to very specific contexts, such as continuing resources ("sequencing pattern," FRBR 4.3.13, p. 38), music ("type of score" and "medium of performance," FRBR 4.3.16–17, p. 38), maps ("scale," "projection," "presentation technique," and "representation of relief," FRBR 4.3.18–21, p. 39), and a few others, any of which might be used to distinguish one expression from another.

On the other hand, some of the attributes appear simply to provide descriptive information that might be recorded about an expression in an expression-level record. These include "extensibility of expression" (FRBR 4.3.6, pp. 36–37), the possibility of content being added later; "revisability of expression" (FRBR 4.3.7, p. 37), the expectation that the expression will be revised later, an attribute that would give a clue to the existence or expected existence of another related expression; "summarization of content" (FRBR 4.3.9, p. 37), lists of chapter titles, for example; "context for the expression" (FRBR 4.3.10, p. 37), a description of the context within which the expression was realized; "critical response to the expression" (FRBR 4.3.11, p. 37); and "use restrictions on the expression" (FRBR 4.3.12, p. 38), a notification that only certain users have rights to view or use the content. These would all be recorded in a database modeled on FRBR in an expression-level record but would not all necessarily serve to distinguish one expression from another.

Note that a few of these attributes might in fact also be appropriately recorded at the work level. For example, "summarization of content" could include plot summaries of works of fiction, which might be recorded at the work level rather than the expression level. Presumably, if the plot of a work changed significantly between expressions, we might consider the result to constitute a new work rather than simply a new expression of the original work. It would seem more efficient to record a plot summary once at the work level rather than repeating it in every expression-level record.

FRAD proposes no additional attributes for the expression entity beyond those already defined in FRBR.

Manifestation

Unlike *expression*, the FRBR entity *manifestation* is a familiar concept, although the term might not be. AACR2/MARC cataloging, for the most part, describes instances of *manifestation. Manifestation* is defined in FRBR as "the physical embodiment of an *expression* of a *work*" (FRBR 3.2.3, p. 20; FRAD 3.4, p. 10). "Embodiment" may sound a bit mystical or even ghoulish—one might think of souls entering bodies—but in this context it simply means an expression of a work that has taken physical form. For example, Homer's *Odyssey* is a work. It has been realized through several different expressions, including an English translation by Alexander Pope. This expression has itself been "embodied" several times, including a 1931 publication by the Limited Editions Club and a 2003 publication by Wildside Press; each of these is a manifestation of this particular expression of the *Odyssey.* Their relationship would be diagrammed in FRBR as in figure 3.8. These two manifestations belong to the same expression of this work because they share the same intellectual content—the text of Pope's 1725 translation.

A manifestation can exist in any physical form. Note here that "physical" includes more ethereal forms such as electronic or digitized content. There are at least two manifestations of the 1999 recording of Debussy's *Syrinx* by Emmanuel Pahud, including one available only electronically, as seen in figure 3.9.

Many people consider the distinction between the expression level and the manifestation level for FRBR Group 1 entities to be essentially a distinction between abstract and concrete: *expression* is abstract, *manifestation* is concrete. In a way this is understandable, since *manifestation* is the level at which an expression first takes on physical form. But *manifestation* is in fact abstract as

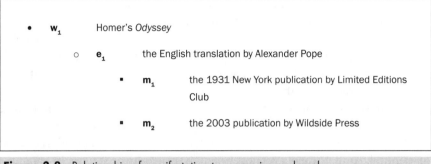

Figure 3.8 Relationship of manifestation to expression and work

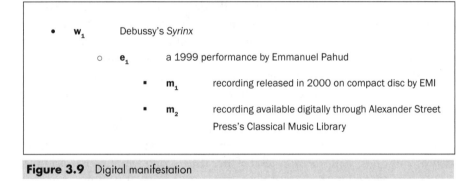

Figure 3.9 Digital manifestation

well. As FRBR puts it, "As an entity, *manifestation* represents all the physical objects that bear the same characteristics, in respect to both intellectual content and physical form." The word "represents" is important: the manifestation itself is not concrete, but it represents something. What it represents is what all the instances of the manifestation have in common, that is, their intellectual content and their physical form in the narrow sense (including aspects such as layout). True, each instance is concrete, but that is a FRBR item, not a manifestation. Even if one could somehow collect every copy of the compact disc released by EMI in 2000 containing the Pahud performance of *Syrinx*, one would not "have" a manifestation; rather, one would have a collection of items, related by the fact that they are from the same manifestation.

The abstract nature of *manifestation* is well shown by current manifestation-level cataloging practices. When we catalog an item in a shared-cataloging environment such as OCLC, we are trying to create a record describing the "ideal" copy of the item we are cataloging; we try to create a record that could be used by any library owning a copy of the item. So if we have a book, say, that is missing a page or has been cut down by an overzealous binder, rather than describe the copy in hand exactly, we attempt to extrapolate the characteristics of the manifestation as a whole when we create the record (or accept somebody else's record). If we only have one volume of a three-volume set, we do not insist that *our* copy represents the true manifestation, but we try as well as we can to describe the item as though it were the ideal copy. But what we are describing here is not any particular, concrete copy but an abstract concept, the manifestation. It is true that in modern publishing practices each copy is often identical or close to identical, so that when a cataloger describes what he or she has in hand, the resulting description *is* representative of all the copies in the manifestation, but the description is still for something abstract: it is a description of what all copies in the publication run have in common, not the details about any particular copy.

FRAD (3.4, p. 10) also comments on the abstract nature of manifestations: "If the embodiment involves the production of multiple copies, the manifestation encompasses the entire set of physical copies produced. In the latter case, the entity described for cataloging purposes is, in effect, an abstraction derived from characteristics of a single copy that are presumed to be shared by all copies in the set that comprises the manifestation."

Note that there can be any number of instances of a particular manifestation, from only one to hundreds of thousands. In the case of an original artwork, there may be only one instance at every level of the FRBR Group 1 entities. For example, Leonardo's *Mona Lisa* is a FRBR work; the artist's original painting is its first expression; the work was embodied in a manifestation when Leonardo put oil on wood; this process created the sole item in this branch of the hierarchy (see figure 3.10). Although there have been many reproductions, these would probably be considered other expressions of the work. For this particular expression there is only one manifestation and one item.

Figure 3.10 assumes that reproductions of artworks in the same medium as the original, though considered the same work, would be different expressions from the original. FRBR is not clear on this point, and it partly depends on how strictly "minor changes" is interpreted (see discussion of *expression,* pp. 27–28). Would the fact that a photographic reproduction of the Mona Lisa is printed on poster board rather than on wood be more than a minor change? Or the fact that oil paints are no longer used? If the reproduction is hand-painted in oil on wood, would this remain the same expression even though inevitably there will be minor differences in strokes? The conclusion might be that reproductions of handmade artworks are by definition different expressions from that of the original.

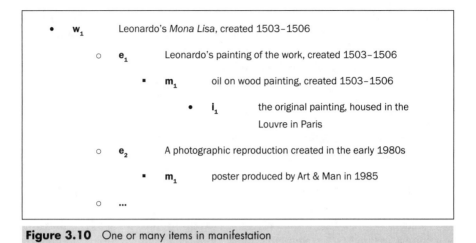

Figure 3.10   One or many items in manifestation

Expression 2 of figure 3.10 has at least one manifestation, the poster produced and being sold by Art & Man. Unlike the original, which exists in one copy, this poster undoubtedly exists in thousands of copies, that is, FRBR items.

Attributes of Manifestation

Thirty-eight attributes have been defined for the entity *manifestation* in FRBR. Most of these defined attributes will not apply to any particular manifestation. Additionally, a given manifestation inherits all the attributes of its expression and work.

Because most current cataloging occurs at a quasi-manifestation level, it is perhaps not surprising that most of the attributes of *manifestation* reflect much of what is recorded in descriptive cataloging.

The first attribution of a manifestation, as of a work and an expression, is "title of the manifestation," defined as "the word, phrase, or group of characters naming the *manifestation*" (FRBR 4.4.1, p. 41). Unlike concepts of uniform title associated with works and expressions, the title of a manifestation would normally be the title or titles associated with the manifestation itself as produced. With a published book, this would include the title as it appears on the title page, as well as any variants found elsewhere in the book (e.g., on the half title, on the spine). In current MARC-based cataloging, this attribute encompasses the sort of title catalogers record in uncontrolled title fields such as 245, 246, and 740. It also includes any title that has been assigned to the manifestation, including key titles and supplied titles (as for a description of an object with no explicit title).

As with *work* and *expression,* "title of the manifestation" is not an attribute of *manifestation* in FRAD. As discussed above under the attribute "title of the work," FRAD considers a manifestation title to be a separate entity, called *name* (see pp. 19–20).

"Statement of responsibility" is the second attribute assigned to *manifestation* (FRBR 4.4.2, pp. 41–42). It may be somewhat surprising that this is not associated with *work* and *expression*—after all, entities are "responsible" for works and expressions as well. Among the Group 1 entities, however, the semiconcrete entity *manifestation* is the first level where an actual statement of responsibility in fact appears. In a work or expression there is no physical place, such as a title page or title frames, for a statement of responsibility to appear. Thus this attribute is defined as "a statement appearing in the *manifestation* . . . that names one or more individuals or groups responsible for the creation or realization of the intellectual or artistic content embodied in the *manifestation.*" For FRBR, this attribute must appear *in* the manifestation in order to be recorded. If no statement of responsibility appears, there is no requirement that one be made up—in fact, unlike AACR2, FRBR has no provision for making up statements of responsibility. On the other hand, FRBR acknowledges that statements of responsibility may not reflect the actual facts about the work or expression embodied in the manifestation: "The stated functions may or may not reflect the actual relationship that exists between the individuals and groups named and the intellectual or artistic content." But even if the statement of responsibility in a given manifestation is false, the statement found is still the statement of responsibility associated with that manifestation and will be recorded as an attribute of the manifestation.

The statement just quoted also points out the importance of the attribute "statement of responsibility" in FRBR by emphasizing the relationships. As an entity-relationship model, FRBR is all about being clear about the relationships between entities. A statement of responsibility is one of the principal sources of information about the relationship between a work or expression embodied in a particular manifestation and its creators. Statements of responsibility are often the only place where information is found about the exact nature of the relationship between a person, corporate body, or family and the work or expression: Is this person the author or the editor? Is that corporate body the producer or simply related in some vague way to the work?

"Edition/issue designation" (FRBR 4.4.3, p. 42; FRAD 4.6, p. 22), like "statement of responsibility," is an attribute defined as a word or phrase appearing *in* the manifestation itself. Statements such as "new and revised edition" are edition designations. It is not clear whether printing statements such as "15th printing" are included in this attribute. By most definitions this would be an "issue designation." On the other hand, does a new printing produced from the same typesetting as a previous one really constitute a separate manifestation? This might be an area where different entities could decide differently. A rare book repository might want to distinguish between printings, whereas a general library might not.

Important to the definition of "edition/issue designation" is that it normally indicates a different manifestation or expression from a related manifestation issued previously by the same publisher or producer. Edition designations of separate publications might have the same wording, but if the publications are produced by different entities, they are not the same manifestation.

Another attribute of *manifestation* is "place of publication/distribution" (FRBR 4.4.4, p. 42; FRAD 4.6, p. 22), the city or town where the manifestation was produced. FRBR acknowledges that there may be more than one place associated with a manifestation. Place of publication as an attribute of *manifestation* is another clue, by the way, that *manifestation* is an abstract concept. Manifestations routinely list more than one place of publication, which simply means that the publisher has offices in many places and the publication was released simultaneously in numerous locations. But the physical item was not produced in all those places at once. It is the abstract concept of publication that occurred in the multiple places.

If FRBR had defined attributes for relationships instead of defining them exclusively for entities, "place of publication/distribution" would probably better be defined as an attribute of the "produced by" relationship inherent between a manifestation and the producing entity. Alternately, since *place* is itself a FRBR entity, the place of publication might better be represented as an entity linked to the manifestation by a relationship such as "published in." This alternate model is diagrammed in figure 3.11.

The attribute "publisher/distributor" is "the individual, group, or organization named in the *manifestation* as being responsible" for the production of the manifestation (FRBR 4.4.5, p. 42; FRAD 4.6, p. 22). As defined, this seems an odd attribute for a manifestation, since a publisher or distributor is an entity itself (person, corporate body, or family) separate from the manifestation and connected to it by the "produced by" relationship. One entity is not an attribute of another entity. Perhaps the authors of FRBR meant something like "publication statement," which, like a statement of responsibility, is an actual statement found *in* the manifestation. As defined, this attribute has some difficult

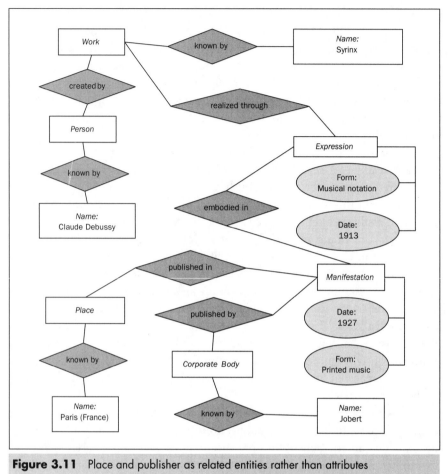

Figure 3.11   Place and publisher as related entities rather than attributes
of manifestation

theoretical problems as well as practical. Would not a FRBR-inspired database more efficiently set up the publisher/distributor as a separate entity linked to the manifestation rather than recording it as an attribute of the manifestation? In the former case one record is made for the publisher or distributor and is linked as often as needed to manifestations; in the latter the publisher or distributor is repeatedly recorded as an attribute of every manifestation entity it is needed for. A model considering "publisher/distributor" an entity rather than an attribute is illustrated in figure 3.11.

The attribute "date of publication/distribution" is the date of public release of the manifestation (FRBR 4.4.6, p. 43; FRAD 4.6, p. 22). Again, this date might more logically be conceived as an attribute of the "produced by" relationship than as an attribute of *manifestation* (see discussion of FRBR 4.2.3 and FRBR 4.3.3 above, pp. 23–25, 30–32).

Another defined attribute of *manifestation* is "fabricator/manufacturer" (FRBR 4.4.7, p. 43). This is the entity "named in the manifestation" that physically produces it. As with "publisher/distributor," since the manufacturer is a FRBR entity itself (a person, corporate body, or family), it seems strange that this should be defined as an attribute of a manifestation. Instead, it is an entity that has a relationship with a manifestation and should so be conceived. Again, perhaps the authors of FRBR intended this attribute to be something like "statement of fabrication or manufacture," but if so it was not well stated.

Oddly, place of fabrication or manufacture is not mentioned as an attribute of *manifestation*, although such places are just as characteristic of manifestations as places of publication. Indeed, physical items contained in a manifestation are associated with a place of manufacture much more concretely than with an abstract place of publication. On the other hand, like "place of publication/ distribution," if anything, the place of manufacture is an attribute of the "produced by" relationship rather than of the entity *manifestation*.[6]

Manifestations often contain a series statement, and so this is another possible attribute of *manifestation* (FRBR 4.4.8, p. 43). "Series statement" is defined as a word or phrase contained in the manifestation indicating that the manifestation is a member of a series.

The attribute "form of carrier" is one of the more important attributes for distinguishing between manifestations (FRBR 4.4.9, p. 43; FRAD 4.6, p. 22). "Carrier" is cataloging jargon for the "medium in which data, sound, images, etc., are stored" (see AACR2 Glossary, "physical carrier"). "Form of carrier" thus refers to the medium in which the expression is embodied, for example, a DVD, an ink-on-paper book, a microfiche, a file residing on a server. If the form of carrier is different between otherwise identical versions of an expression, this automatically means that we have two separate manifestations. FRBR does note that a complex manifestation can have more than one physical carrier associated with it, as with a novel accompanied by a compact disc. In this case the "form of carrier" attribute comprises all the physical carriers associated with the manifestation. Differences still indicate a different manifestation. A novel issued with a compact disc containing a performance of the novel and the identical novel issued with an LP containing the same performance are different manifestations, although they are manifestations of the same expression of the work.

The attribute "extent of the carrier" (FRBR 4.4.10, p. 43) is roughly equivalent to the concept of "extent statement" given in current cataloging practices and describes the number of physical units making up the carrier of the manifestation. Examples include number of volumes or cassettes in a set and number of pages in a book. "Extent of carrier" does not include such concepts as length of a sound recording or number of words or letters printed in a book; these are attributes of expressions (FRBR 4.3.8, p. 43).

"Physical medium" (FRBR 4.4.11, p. 44) is not the same attribute as "form of carrier." The physical medium is the actual material the carrier is composed of. For example, the physical medium of a compact disc might be plastic or, rarely, a metal of some sort. The physical medium of a book might include paper, cardboard, glue, thread, and cloth. Included in the physical medium are all the components, even inks and paints. This is sometimes an important attribute for distinguishing one manifestation from another, but it is rarely recorded in current cataloging practices except in some specialist applications such as manuscript or graphic materials cataloging.

"Capture mode"—the means used to record notation, sound, or images— seems somewhat esoteric, but it is another attribute that can be used to distinguish between otherwise identical versions of an expression (FRBR 4.4.12, p. 44). For example, an analog production and a digital production of the same performance would result in two manifestations. Presumably this attribute could apply to the difference between information captured by "ink on paper" and a PDF file showing the same page but projected on a computer screen—a different "means used to record [the] notation."

"Dimensions of the carrier" (FRBR 4.4.13, p. 44) corresponds to statements of dimensions in current cataloging practice. It refers to the physical dimensions of the carrier, which may include the container if there is one.

"Manifestation identifier" (FRBR 4.4.14, p. 44) is "a number or code uniquely associated with the *manifestation* that serves to differentiate that *manifestation* from any other *manifestation*." A manifestation can have more than one manifestation identifier. The important factor is that this identifier uniquely differentiates a manifestation from other manifestations.

ISBN is the most prominent example of a manifestation identifier for books, ISSN for serials. ISBN is not without problems as a manifestation identifier. The ISBN system was not set up with FRBR in mind, so publishers assigning ISBNs are not always careful, to say the least, to assign new ISBNs only to new manifestations. It is not uncommon, particularly in European publishing practice, to find an otherwise identical book assigned a new ISBN after a few years. Does this constitute a new manifestation? Perhaps so.

A given manifestation may legitimately have more than one ISBN. For example, ISBNs are typically assigned to each volume of a multivolume set. Since the manifestation comprises all the parts, in this instance a manifestation might have more than one ISBN associated with it.

In current cataloging practice it is also common to include more than one ISBN in a bibliographic record—popularly supposed to correspond to a FRBR manifestation record—for similar versions of the expression, such as a hardback and paperback copy of a publication issued at the same time. A strict interpretation of FRBR would indicate that these are different manifestations since they have different physical medium attributes (FRBR 4.4.11, p. 44).

These fourteen attributes are the most important as distinguishing characteristics between manifestations. Others are useful in more specialized situations. For instance, "typeface," "type size," "foliation," and "collation" (FRBR 4.4.18–21, pp. 45–46) are useful for distinguishing between various manifestations of early printed books, especially when the collecting entity is a rare book collector. More general collectors might not find such distinctions useful or, more likely, would not have the means or resources to do the research necessary to employ such distinguishing characteristics.

Nevertheless, notwithstanding the rather specialized nature of most of the later attributes defined, all of them are characteristics that distinguish between manifestations. If given versions of an expression differ in one or more of the manifestation attributes, more than likely the versions are different manifestations.

FRAD does not propose any additional attributes for manifestation beyond those already defined in FRBR.

Item

A FRBR *item* is a single instance or exemplar of the entity *manifestation* (FRBR 3.2.4, p. 22; FRAD 3.4, p. 10). At this level of FRBR, we leave the abstract realm and enter the concrete. An item is physical. It can be a single object (one compact disc, one computer file) or more than one object (all the volumes of the *Encyclopaedia Britannica,* all the "pages" contained within a discrete website). The FRBR entity *item* usually corresponds to the informal notion of a copy. When I say my library owns a copy of Pope's translation of the *Odyssey,* in FRBR terms I might mean it owns one item (numbered 797) of a particular manifestation (the 1931 publication by Limited Editions Club) of a particular expression (Pope's 1725 translation) of a particular work (Homer's *Iliad*). This would be diagrammed as in figure 3.12.

The chief relationship the FRBR entity *item* has with other FRBR entities is the "owned by" relationship (FRBR figure 3.2, p. 14), but there are certainly other

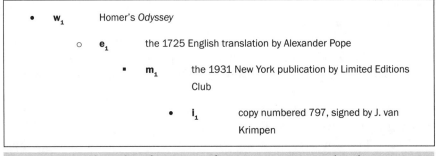

Figure 3.12 Relationship of item to manifestation, expression, and work

relationship types (e.g., "borrowed by," "donated by," "sold by") that could exist between an item and another FRBR entity such as a person or corporate body, any of which relationships might be of interest in a bibliographic database.

Attributes of Item

In modern publishing practices, items are rarely distinguished from each other by handwritten numbers inked onto the last page like the copy of the *Odyssey* diagrammed in figure 3.12. But they do have distinguishing characteristics. These are found in the attributes defined for *item*. These are fewer than those defined for *work, expression,* and *manifestation,* but bear in mind that a Group 1 entity inherits the attributes of all the entities above it. Thus in the example illustrated in figure 3.12, "English" is an attribute of the expression (FRBR 4.3.4, p. 36), but by inheritance it is also an attribute of the manifestation and the item. Extent, such as "548 p.," is an attribute of *manifestation* (FRBR 4.4.10, p. 43), but this is usually by inheritance also an attribute of an item within the manifestation, assuming it has not been damaged in some way. Changes can occur after the production process is complete, such as rebinding or mutilation; this does not result in a new manifestation but is simply an attribute of the item (FRBR 3.2.3, p. 22).

Nine attributes have been assigned to the entity *item* in FRBR. The first is "item identifier" (FRBR 4.5.1, p. 49), a number or code that uniquely differentiates the item not only from other items within a manifestation but from all other items owned by the owning entity. The item identifier can be something like a barcode or RFID tag. Call number is mentioned as an example of item identifier, but call number often does not uniquely distinguish between items, for instance, when an institution owns more than one copy of the same item, unless the copy designation ("copy 1," "copy 2," etc.) is a part of the call number. The item illustrated in figure 3.13 has an item identifier (the number on a barcode) that is different from all other item identifiers used by the owning institution.

It should be noted that FRAD defines a separate entity, *identifier,* with which there may be some overlap with the attribute "item identifier." The FRAD entity *identifier* is defined as "a number, code . . . , etc. that is uniquely associated with an entity" (FRAD 3.4, p. 13). A barcode number, for example, is in fact a number "uniquely associated with an entity," the item. The FRAD identifier is, however, much broader; it can be applied to any FRBR entity, not just any item.

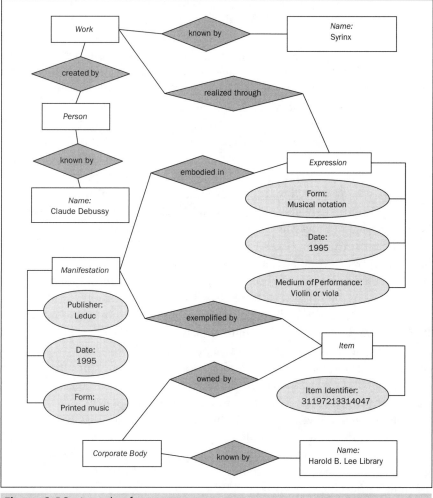

Figure 3.13 Item identifier

The second attribute of *item* given is "fingerprint" (FRBR 4.5.2, p. 49). This is defined as "an identifier constructed by combining groups of characters transcribed from specified pages of a printed *item*." This is true. Evidence used in constructing a fingerprint is indeed gathered from the pages of a printed item. But the next statement in the definition, that "the technique is used primarily to signal differences between individual copies of early printed books," is incorrect and demonstrates a misunderstanding of fingerprints. Fingerprint, as defined in *Descriptive Cataloging of Rare Materials (Books),* is "a group of characters selected from specific locations in the publication, which, when combined with the date of publication, etc., serves to identify a book as having been printed from a certain setting of type."[7] Books printed from different settings of type belong to different manifestations. They are not different items within a single manifestation. Items can share the same fingerprint if they all come from the same setting of type (i.e., they are all items within the same manifestation). A fingerprint does not distinguish between items (copies). If used as a FRBR attribute, "fingerprint" should be considered an attribute of *manifestation,* not of *item.*

"Provenance of the item" is a record of previous ownership of the item (FRBR 4.5.3, p. 49). The provenance could be as simple as the publisher of the item if the owning entity is the first to purchase the item. This sort of provenance is probably not too useful in identifying a particular item. By contrast, in specialist situations such as rare book collecting, provenance can be quite detailed and important for identifying a particular copy or item. A scholar investigating Alexander Pope's translation process might well be extremely interested in examining the copy of Homer's *Iliad* in Greek that once belonged to Alexander Pope, containing the translator's annotations. For such a scholar the "provenance of the item" attribute, used to identify a specific FRBR item, becomes quite important.

"Marks/inscriptions" (FRBR 4.5.4, p. 49) is also important for identifying an individual item. Although specialist applications seem most obvious, as in the Pope example just cited, this attribute actually applies to nearly all items within a manifestation, even with quite modern publications. Owners often mark items they own in some way, whether signing or stamping a book or affixing a call number or barcode. Even electronic items housed in servers are marked in some way, identifying the rights of an owning entity to access the item.

The five remaining attributes are not as important for distinguishing one item from another, but as attributes they certainly are appropriate to the FRBR entity *item* rather than one of those higher in the hierarchy. Individual items, not whole manifestations, are found in exhibitions (FRBR 4.5.5, p. 50); have a condition (a missing page, etc.) (FRBR 4.5.6, p. 50); or have been or will be treated (e.g., restoration of a film) (FRBR 4.5.7, p. 50). Access restrictions (FRBR

4.5.9, p. 50) can occur at either the item level or the manifestation level (see FRBR 4.4.17, p. 45). At the item level, a restriction might be imposed on a particular copy; for instance, an institution might allow handling of a very brittle book only under restricted conditions. At the manifestation level, copying of any item in an entire manifestation might be restricted because of copyright laws.

FRAD defines only one attribute associated with items, "location of item" (FRAD 4.7, p. 23). This is defined as the collection or institution in which the item is held or made available.

Person

Person is the first of the FRBR Group 2 entities. Group 2 entities "represent those responsible for the intellectual or artistic content, the physical production and dissemination, or custodianship of the entities in the first group" (FRBR 3.1.2, p. 13). *Person* is defined simply as "an individual," presumably human, living or dead (FRBR 3.2.5, p. 25). FRAD (3.4, p. 8) expands this definition to encompass "an individual or a persona established or adopted by an individual or group." "Persona" in this context allows for individual and joint pseudonyms.

Person is defined in FRBR only to the extent that this entity can participate in the creation or realization of a work or is the subject of a work. This limitation given in FRBR 3.2.5 seems unnecessarily confining, particularly since in FRBR figure 3.2 persons are shown to have a potential relationship with any Group 1 entity, not just with works and expressions.

Although not mentioned in FRBR, in addition to relationships with Group 1 entities, persons can also have relationships with other Group 2 entities. A person may write under different pseudonyms. Under current cataloging practice (and FRBR does not forbid this), such pseudonyms are considered to represent different entities, but there is obviously a strong relationship between these entities. Similarly, persons have relationships with corporate bodies and families. It might be advisable in a FRBR entity-relationship database to link person records with corporate body records, for example, for a member of a musical group. Obviously persons have nonbibliographic relationships with other persons as well, such as sibling or marital relationships. Such relationships might be of interest but might not be considered essential relationships to bring out in a bibliographic database.

Relationships between persons and other persons, corporate bodies, or families are discussed in FRAD 5.3 (pp. 31–35).

Persons can also have relationships with Group 3 entities (topics). Edith Piaf is best known as a French singer and was also an actress and writer, all possible

Group 3 concept entities. It would probably be useful to database users if a link were made relating the person entity record for Edith Piaf with the concept entity record for "Singers," "Actresses," or "Authors, French." If such linkages were consistently made between Group 2 and Group 3 entity records, a user of the database could make a query under "Actresses," for example, and find links not only to works about actresses (relationships between Group 1 and Group 3 entities) but also to the person entity records for individual actresses (relationships between Group 2 and Group 3 entities). This person entity record would, in turn, link to records for works or other Group 1 entities by or about the person or having some other relationship with the person.

The closest equivalent to recording the entity *person* in current cataloging practice is the creation of personal name authority records. Like the FRBR entity *person,* the entity recorded in personal name authority records is independent of "any particular *expression* or *manifestation* of a *work,*" and these authority records "enable us to name and identify the individual in a consistent manner." Indeed, current authority records may constitute a stepping stone to a true FRBR entity record for persons in an entity-relationship database. The existence of large numbers of authority records for persons may make the transformation of our catalogs to FRBR entity-relationship databases easier.

Attributes of Person

The first and most important attribute of *person* is "name of person" (FRBR 4.6.1, p. 51). The name is any word, character, or phrase by which a person is known. FRBR notes that a person may be known by more than one name, or by more than one form of the same name. This is a familiar concept to anyone who has dealt with authority work. FRBR also asserts that a bibliographic agency "normally selects one of those names as the uniform heading for purposes of consistency in naming and referencing the *person.*" In current cataloging practices this is true and absolutely necessary to prevent chaos in the catalog. In an entity-relationship database, however, this might not be necessary. In such a database a single record would exist for each person, linked as appropriate to other FRBR entities. The person record would contain as the (repeatable) "name of person" attribute all names and variants of names associated with the person entity being recorded. Unlike current practice, where we follow rules to determine the "authorized" form of the name, it might not be necessary in a FRBR person entity record to decide that one of the "name of person" attributes is more authoritative than another. A user of such a database would simply find her way to the person record by searching for any of the recorded forms; once to the record, she would find through the linkages the work, expression, manifestation, item, or other entity records related to the person entity she found—and it would not matter which name she started out with.

"Name of person" is not an attribute of *person* in FRAD. As discussed under the attribute "title of the work" (see pp. 18–20), FRAD considers the name of the person to be a separate entity, called *name*. Figure 3.13, for example, includes a person entity related to a name entity following the FRAD model. Figure 3.3a shows the treatment of "name of person" in the FRBR model.

"Dates of person" is the second attribute of the entity *person* (FRBR 4.6.2, p. 51; FRAD 4.1, p. 16, there called "dates associated with the person"). This normally means the dates during which a person was alive or, if unknown, the dates during which a person was active in a particular activity (e.g., as an author; for an example, see figure 3.6). This is a descriptive attribute and is useful in distinguishing between persons who have the same name.

The third defined person attribute is "title of person" (FRBR 4.6.3, p. 51; FRAD 4.1, p. 16). "Title" here has the sense of a word or phrase associated with a person, such as "Dr." or "General." Like "dates of person," "title of person" is a descriptive attribute useful to distinguish between persons who have the same name. It is somewhat less useful than "dates of person" for this purpose, however, because it is less predictable. A person's birth and death dates are facts that for the most part may be ascertained. In contrast, a person may have many titles or variants on the same title. Presumably in an entity-relationship database, all titles could be listed as an attribute of the person, but a multiplicity of titles might detract from the main purpose of the attribute, to identify the person and distinguish him or her from others with the same name.

The final attribute of person is "other designation associated with the person" (FRBR 4.6.4, p. 51; FRAD 4.1, p. 16), a sort of grab bag allowing other designations useful to distinguish the person from others to be recorded as an attribute.

There are likely many other attributes of the entity *person* that would be recorded in a person record in a FRBR entity-relationship database. These are not covered in FRBR, but many of them are covered in FRAD, the extension of FRBR that works out the functional requirements of authority data. These include "gender," "place of birth," "place of death," "country" (a country with which the person is identified), "place of residence," "language of person," and "field of activity" (FRAD 4.1, pp. 17–18). Any of these would be helpful to the user of the database in identifying a particular person.

Corporate Body

The entity *corporate body* is "an organization or group of individuals and/or orga-nizations acting as a unit" (FRBR 3.2.6, p. 24; FRAD 3.4, p. 8). This is more or less the same definition as that used in current cataloging practice. Included is any organization or group identified by a particular name, including meetings and similar events, as well as jurisdictional corporate bodies (e.g., countries, cities).

The same limitation is expressed in FRBR for corporate bodies as for persons, that they are treated as entities "only to the extent that they are involved in the creation or realization of a *work* . . . or are the subject of a *work*." As with persons, this limitation seems unnecessarily confining. Corporate bodies can in a bibliographic database have relationships with any Group 1 entity. And as with persons, corporate bodies can have relationships with other Group 2 entities. Examples are predecessor and successor bodies, or persons who are members of the corporate body. Similarly, corporate bodies can have relationships with Group 3 entities. For example, the corporate body entity "Peter, Paul, and Mary" has a relationship to the concept entity "folk musicians" (see fuller discussion above, under "Person").

As with persons, current cataloging practice has a near equivalent to the FRBR corporate body entity record in authority records for corporate bodies. These enable us to "name and identify the organization or group in a consistent manner, independently of how the name of the organization or group appears on or in any particular *expression* or *manifestation* of a *work*."

Attributes of Corporate Body

Five attributes have been defined in FRBR for *corporate body*. The first is "name of the corporate body" (FRBR 4.7.1, p. 52). This is the word, phrase, or character(s) by which a body is known. Like persons, corporate bodies can be known by more than one name or more than one form of the same name. As FRBR notes, a bibliographic agency normally selects one of these names as a uniform heading for purposes of consistency. This is a statement of current practice. It might not carry over to a true entity-relationship environment, where it might not be as important or desirable to choose one of the names as the authorized form, as we saw above for "name of person" (see pp. 48–49).

Note that in AACR2 by definition a corporate body must have a name—groups of persons that do not have a collective name are not considered corporate bodies (AACR2 21.1B1). Since "name of the corporate body" is the first-stated corporate body attribute in FRBR, presumably this requirement (that a body be named) applies under FRBR as well. This is less clear in FRAD, in which "name" is not an attribute of corporate bodies but rather an entity itself with a relationship to corporate bodies. Since no relationships are required in FRAD, it is not clear whether or not the authors of FRAD think that a corporate body must have a name (see further discussion of this issue under "Attributes of Work," pp. 18–20). For an example of the relationship of *corporate body* to *name* following the FRAD model, see figure 3.13.

"Number associated with the corporate body" (FRBR 4.7.2, p. 52) is mainly used with recurring meetings or events (e.g., 55th Annual Conference of the Cardiological Society of India). This attribute allows a meeting to be distinguished from other meetings with the same name. "Number" is not an attribute of *corporate body* in FRAD because it is included in the definition of a distinct FRAD entity, *name* (FRAD 3.4, p. 13).

A third attribute of corporate body is "place associated with the corporate body" (FRBR 4.7.3, p. 52; FRAD 4.3, p. 18). This is a location with which the corporate body is associated. It is usually a jurisdictional name (e.g., Seattle, Washington); with meeting names the place is sometimes the name of a hosting institution, such as Purdue University for the 62nd Purdue Pest Control Conference.

An obvious problem with recording place as an attribute of corporate bodies is choice of the place name. Many corporate bodies are associated with many places. Should the "place" attribute record the place associated with the corporate body's headquarters? The area it serves? Perhaps more than one place might be recorded for this attribute.

Another possible problem in the FRBR/FRAD model is considering "place" an attribute of the entity *corporate body* instead of considering it an entity in its own right linked to the entity *corporate body* through a relationship. *Place* is in fact a defined FRBR/FRAD entity. In a fully worked-out entity-relationship scheme, considering it so in a relationship with a corporate body rather than as an attribute of a corporate body might turn out to be a preferable arrangement.

Except for meeting names, the attribute "place associated with the corporate body" is not regularly recorded in authority records for corporate bodies, but it certainly seems a useful attribute (or relationship to bring out) that should be expected in a FRBR corporate body entity record.

"Date associated with the corporate body" (FRBR 4.7.4, p. 53; FRAD 4.3, p. 18) is fairly broadly defined. For meetings it is the date or range of dates when the meeting was held. For other corporate bodies it is any date associated with the corporate body. This might include the range of dates during which the body was in existence, or the date the body was established. Like the "place" attribute, current practice regularly records this information in corporate body authority records only for meetings or if a date or dates are needed to distinguish one corporate body from another with the same name. It does seem that it would be useful to record this information more regularly as one of the attributes in the corporate body entity record.

"Other designation associated with the corporate body" (FRBR 4.7.5, p. 52; FRAD 4.3, p. 18) is the last defined attribute in FRBR for *corporate body,* and like the final FRBR attribute for *person* (FRBR 4.6.4, p. 51) it fills a necessary niche. There are times when none of the other attributes or combinations of attributes suffice to distinguish between different corporate bodies.

There are other possible attributes for the entity *corporate body* that might be recorded in a corporate body entity record. These are more fully worked out in FRAD and include "type of corporate body," a general characterization such as "government body" or "conference"; "language of the corporate body," the language the body uses in its communications; and "field of activity," the area or areas the body is engaged in or has responsibility for. Each of these three FRAD attributes could also be conceived as entities (probably concept entities) with a relationship to corporate body entities. More clearly attributes are two other FRAD attributes: "address," the address of the body's office(s); and "history," information pertaining to the history of the body (FRAD 4.3, p. 19).

Family

A third Group 2 entity, not found in FRBR, is defined in FRAD. *Family* is defined as "two or more persons related by birth, marriage, adoption, or similar legal status, or [who] otherwise present themselves as a family" (FRAD 3.4, p. 8).

This is fairly new territory in cataloging practice. AACR2 does not recognize *family* as an entity that can be used in descriptive cataloging. Family names, however, have been used in subject cataloging for some time and have also been used in archival cataloging as main and added entry points.[8] They will also be included for use in descriptive cataloging in RDA.[9] The ability to consider families as entities that can be linked to FRBR Group 1 entities in creator or producer relationships will be welcome to many other communities. RDA presumably will include more fully developed guidelines for formation and use of family names.[10]

Attributes of Family

FRAD defines four attributes for the entity *family* (FRAD 4.2, p. 18): "type of family," a description of the family type, for example, "clan" or "dynasty"; "dates of family," any dates associated with the family; "places associated with family," for example, where the family resided or had some connection (as noted above for corporate bodies, this attribute might instead be seen as a separate entity with a relationship to families); and "history of family," any information about the history of the family.

"Name of family" is not given as one of the attributes of *family* in FRAD, because there *name* is treated as a separate entity rather than as an attribute of the various entities (see discussion above under "Attributes of Work," pp. 18–20). Presumably, if *family* had been defined as an entity in FRBR, "name of family" would have been the first defined attribute, as with the other entities.

Group 3 Entities: Concept, Object, Event, and Place

The Group 3 entities serve as subjects of works (FRBR 3.1.3, p. 16). Group 1 and 2 entities can also serve as subjects of works; the distinction is that the *only* relationship a Group 3 entity can have with a work is as a subject.

The first of the four FRBR Group 3 entities is *concept,* defined as "an abstract notion or idea" (FRBR 3.2.7, p. 25; FRAD 3.4, p. 11). FRBR points out that the entity *concept* encompasses the whole field of human knowledge and that it may be very broad or very narrow. As with all the entities, FRBR brings in the idea of authority work when it indicates that defining an instance of the entity enables us to name the concept in a consistent manner, even if an expression or manifestation of the work being described does not contain the name of the concept.

FRBR does not mention this, but a concept can also serve as the subject of an expression, a manifestation, or even in rare cases an item. FRBR also omits a discussion of genre/form as an entity. Genre/form could be considered a subclass of the concept *entity,* since all genre/form terms can also be used as topical terms. The usage could be distinguished by the relationship type. Alternately, genre/form could be considered an entity separate from *concept* (see fuller discussion of these problems under "Work," pp. 20–22).

The entity *object* is defined as "a material thing," contrasting with *concept,* which is abstract (FRBR 3.2.8, p. 26; FRAD 3.4, p. 11). Objects can be things that exist in nature, such as oak trees or whales, or things that are created by humans, such as the Golden Gate Bridge or the pyramids of Egypt. It should be pointed out that the entity *object,* since it is a Group 3 entity, excludes anything that might be considered to have a Group 2 (creator) relationship with a work, expression, manifestation, or item. Thus under current cataloging practice a ship, although certainly an object in the sense of a material thing, is considered capable of authorship as a corporate body (e.g., of the ship's log) and so is considered a corporate body, not an object. Similarly, a shopping center, though a building or collection of buildings, is also considered a corporate body (see *Subject Cataloging Manual* H405). Such distinctions are obviously subject to interpretation, which will vary from culture to culture and from time period to time period.

Also explicitly excluded from the entity *object* in FRAD are humans, although other "animate objects occurring in nature" such as nonhuman mammals and plants are included (FRAD 3.4, p. 11). Again, this is because humans are Group 2 entities. Trees and elephants are not considered capable of having creator or producer relationships with FRBR Group 1 entities.

The FRBR entity *event* is defined as "an action or occurrence" (FRBR 3.2.9, p. 27; FRAD 3.4, p. 11). This comprises all kinds of events, natural or human-created. Examples range from the eruption of Vesuvius in AD 79 to the stock market crash of 1987. Excluded are "events" that are considered capable of FRBR Group 2 (creator) relationships with Group 1 entities. Under current cataloging practice, these include events such as athletic contests (e.g., the Olympic Games), other types of competitions or contests, named events such as fairs or exhibitions, and expeditions (see *Subject Cataloging Manual* H405). As with the entity *object,* distinctions of this type are subject to interpretation, and individual instances of the entity might slide back and forth between *event* and *corporate body* depending on the culture or the time period.

FRAD is somewhat confusing on this point, since it states that included in events are "meetings, sporting events, expeditions, etc." (FRAD 3.4, p. 11), whereas among corporate bodies it includes "groups that are constituted as meetings, conferences, congresses, expeditions, exhibitions, festivals, fairs, etc." (FRAD 3.4, pp. 8–9). FRAD acknowledges that "cataloguing rules may differ with respect to the treatment of meetings, etc. In some instances they may be treated simply as events, but in other instances they may be treated as corporate bodies" (FRAD 3.4, p. 11).

Place, the final defined entity in FRBR, is defined simply as "a location" (FRBR 3.2.10, p. 27; FRAD 3.4, p. 12). This includes all kinds of locations, both on and below land, outside the earth, anywhere in the universe (and perhaps beyond?). What the entity might not include is locations whose names also double as jurisdictions, that is, a Group 2 entity (corporate body). In current cataloging practice, because "Arizona" is the name for both the government (jurisdiction) and the geographic area (location), both concepts are included in its authority record, which is coded in MARC authorities format as a geographic name (X51).

When used in the bibliographic record, the name is coded as a geographic name (651) when used as the subject of a work but as a corporate body (110/710) when representing the jurisdiction in an authorial capacity. A single authority record controls the heading, whether it is used to represent the jurisdiction or the location. This confusing situation might continue in a FRBR-based entity-relationship database.

Alternately, it might make sense in such a database to have one record for the Group 2 entity "Arizona" (the jurisdiction) and a separate record for the Group 3 entity "Arizona" (the location). In this way, works about the government of Arizona could be linked to the Group 2 entity record, and works about the natural history of the state or its mineral resources could be linked to the Group 3 entity record. This might make more sensible organization of search results than our current practice, which lumps these two separate concepts (jurisdiction and location) together in a single authority record. This is apparently the direction envisioned in FRAD, which includes in the explanation of the entity *place* the statement that it "includes geo-political jurisdictions (i.e., geographic territories governed by political authorities)" (FRAD 3.4, p. 12). This carefully worded statement appears to bring the geographic territory into the entity *place* while excluding the government itself, which would be a corporate body. The FRAD discussion of *corporate body* indicates that the entity "includes organizations that act as territorial authorities, exercising or claiming to exercise government functions over a certain territory" (FRAD 3.4, p. 9). Thus under the FRAD model it appears that the concept of jurisdictional authority is split off from the concept of geopolitical jurisdiction, a departure from current practice.

Attributes of Concept, Object, Event, and Place

Concept, object, event, and *place* have only one attribute each in FRBR, "term for the concept" (FRBR 4.8.1, p. 53), "term for the object" (FRBR 4.9.1, p. 54), "term for the event" (FRBR 4.10.1, p. 54), and "term for the place" (FRBR 4.11.1, pp. 54–55). This is a word or phrase used to name the concept, object, event, or place. FRBR recognizes that more than one term in a given language might designate such an entity. And of course in a database with users speaking more than one language, a Group 3 entity would have different terms based on language as well. As FRBR points out, currently bibliographic agencies normally choose one of these terms as a uniform heading. In a true entity-relationship database, designating just one of the terms in the entity record as "uniform" or "authoritative" might not be necessary, since the term would not be found in all the related FRBR Group 1 entity records but only in the single Group 3 entity record for the concept connected to the Group 1 entity records by the relationship link. In such a database, the user could reach the concept, object, event, or place entity record by any of the variant terms in any language recorded in its entity record and be led to all other related entities.

FRAD adds several attributes to these entities:

To *concept* it adds the attribute "type of concept," defined as "a categorization or generic descriptor for the concept" (FRAD 4.8, p. 23).

To *object* it adds five attributes (FRAD 4.9, p. 23): "type of object," like the attribute of *concept* "a categorization or generic descriptor for the object"; "date of production," the date the object was produced; "place of production," the city, town, or other locality associated with the production of the object; "producer/fabricator," the individual or group responsible for the production of the object; and "physical medium," the material from which the object is produced. Of these five, "type of object," "place of production," "producer/fabricator," and "physical medium" could all be conceived as separate entities related to the entity *object* rather than as attributes of *object.*

To *event* two attributes are added (FRAD 4.10, p. 24): "date associated with the event" and "place associated with the event." Both of these attributes explicitly are geared toward meetings, conferences, exhibitions, fairs, and so on, although they would certainly apply to natural events such as storms, volcanic eruptions, and the like. In FRBR these attributes are associated with corporate bodies (FRBR 4.7.2–3, p. 52).

FRAD adds two attributes to the entity *place* (FRAD 4.11, p. 24): "coordinates" and "other geographical information." In FRBR, "coordinates" is an attribute of *work* (FRBR 4.2.11, pp. 34–35).

Name

Several entities specific to FRAD are not given as entities in FRBR: *name, identifier, controlled access point, agency,* and *rules.*

In FRBR, "name" (or in some cases the equivalent "title") is the first attribute of each entity. This makes intuitive sense, so it may surprise readers of FRAD that none of the equivalent FRAD entities have the "name" attribute. Instead, in FRAD, *name* is an entity. This is because for the FRAD model it is necessary to have the entity *name* to link each FRBR entity with its controlled access point, another defined entity in FRAD (see figure 3.14; see also figure 3.2, where this is schematized for the entity *work*). It is not clear how practical considering name as a separate entity rather than as an attribute would be in designing a bibliographic database, but diagramming throughout this book is based on the FRAD model.

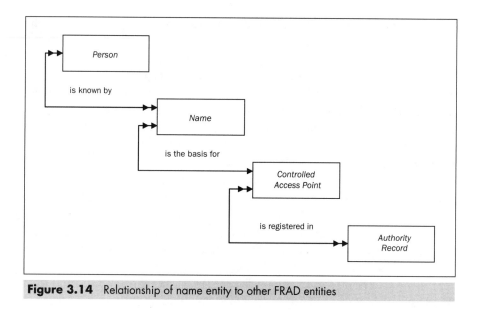

Figure 3.14   Relationship of name entity to other FRAD entities

Name is defined in FRAD as "a character or group of words and/or characters by which an entity is known" (FRAD 3.4, p. 12). FRAD does not clarify exactly how a name would be treated as an entity. In the case of a person, would a complete name be used as an instance of the entity, such as "Bill Clinton"? Or would "Bill" be one instance of the entity and "Clinton" another?[11] What about "William Jefferson Clinton"? Is this form a separate entity from the "Bill Clinton" instance of the name? The positioning of the double arrows in figures 3.2 and 3.14, based on FRAD figures 4 and 5 (pp. 62–63), shows that an instance of the FRBR entity (e.g., person) can be linked to more than one FRAD name entity. Conversely, the FRAD name entity can be linked to more than one FRBR person entity.

Attributes of Name

Name has six attributes in FRAD (FRAD 4.12, pp. 24–25):

"Type of name" is the broad category into which the name falls, such as personal name, corporate name, or family name. As it is useful in current catalog databases to be able to differentiate authority records by broad categories of this sort, so in a FRBR/FRAD-based database this attribute would be useful in helping distinguish between different types of the name entity.

"Scope of usage" refers to the form of work associated with a particular name, for example, literary works or detective novels. This attribute seems out of place for the name entity, since a particular instance of a name can be shared by more than one person. The attribute is more appropriately associated with the person entity.

"Dates of usage" are the dates associated with the use of the name, such as the period in which a person used a pseudonym, or the date a person changed names because of an event like marriage. Like "scope of usage," this attribute seems more appropriate to a person entity than to a name, since an instance of a name can be shared by more than one person. Even better, it could be defined as an attribute of the "known by" relationship, if FRBR/FRAD defined attributes for relationships.

"Language of name" is the language in which the name is expressed. For example, this attribute for the name "Livy" would be English, and the name "Titus Livius," associated with the same person, would be Latin.

"Script of name" refers to the script in which the name is rendered. This will become important as catalogs and other databases begin to display and search more languages with non-Latin alphabets.

"Transliteration scheme of name" refers to the scheme used to produce a transliterated form of the name. For instance, the name "Mao Tse-tung" is a result of the Wade-Giles transliteration scheme, whereas "Mao Zedong," representing the same person and in fact the same name, is a Pinyin scheme transliteration. FRAD does not comment on whether these two forms represent a single instance of the name entity or whether they would be considered two separate instances.

Interestingly enough, the words themselves constituting a name (e.g., "Bill" and "Clinton") are not defined in FRAD as an attribute of the name.

Figure 3.15 illustrates the FRAD entity *name* worked out for four persons related to the name "Larry King." Four instances of the entity *person* are represented and three instances of the entity *name*. It will be seen that the first name, "Lawrence P. King," is related to two persons; the second, "Larry King," is related to three; and the third, "Lawrence Harvey Ziegler," is related to only one. Conversely, two of the persons, the sociologist and the composer, are related to only one name, whereas the other two are each related to two different instances of the name, though not the same two.

Identifier

The entity *identifier* is defined as "a number, code, word, phrase, logo, device, etc., that is uniquely associated with an entity, and serves to differentiate that entity from other entities within the domain in which the identifier is assigned" (FRAD 3.4, p. 13). Among these are numbers such as identification numbers assigned by governments to persons or corporate bodies, standard identifiers assigned by reg-

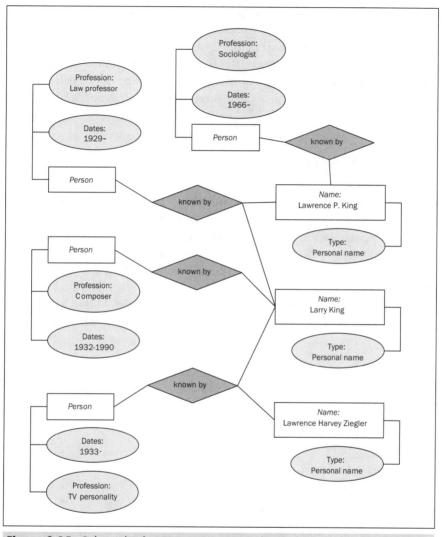

Figure 3.15 Relationship between name entity and person entity in FRAD

istration authorities (e.g., the publisher's prefix in the ISBN string), and thematic index numbers assigned by others than the composer to musical works (numbers such as opus numbers assigned by the composer are considered in FRAD an attribute of *work* called "numeric designation"; FRAD 4.4, p. 20). Explicitly excluded from identifiers are record numbers assigned to authority records. It is not clear why this is so.

Note that there is a slight overlap between this FRAD entity and an attribute of the FRBR entity *item*, "item identifier" (see p. 45).

Figure 3.16, based on FRAD figures 2 (p. 7) and 4–5 (pp. 62–63), illustrates for the entity *work* how *identifier* relates to other FRAD entities. Note from the positions of the double and single arrows that, whereas the work can have more than one identifier, the identifier can theoretically have a relationship with only one work.

Attributes of Identifier

Three attributes have been assigned to *identifier* (FRAD 4.13, p. 25): "Type of identifier" is the broad classification indicating the type of identifier, such as ISBN. "Identifier string" is the sequence of characters or graphic designs (e.g., logos) that make up the identifier. "Suffix" is a character or set of characters appended to the identifier string; a familiar example is the check character at the end of the ISBN, which allows the machine to verify that the number has been structured correctly.

Figure 3.17 illustrates a specific instance of an identifier. Mozart's opera *The Magic Flute* is referred to by the number 620 (usually cited as K. 620), the number

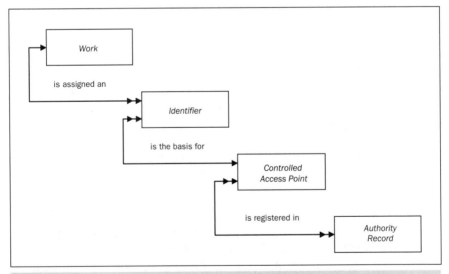

Figure 3.16   Relationship of identifier entity to other FRAD entities

assigned to it in the standard bibliography of the composer's complete works.[12] Note that the identifier is linked to the work record by an "assigned" relationship. The work record is linked to two name records by a "known by" relationship and is also linked with a person record by a "created by" relationship.

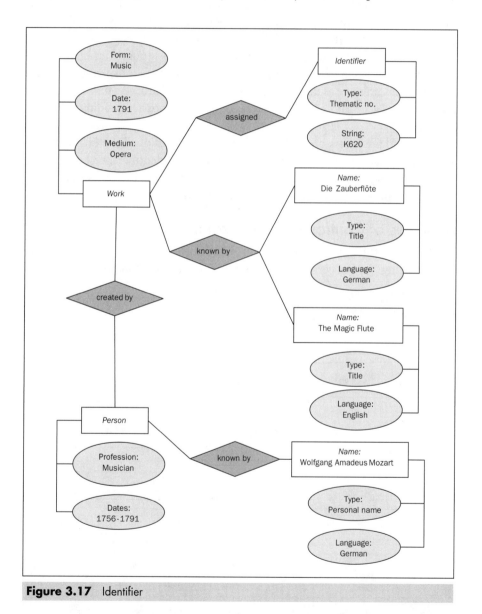

Figure 3.17 Identifier

Controlled Access Point

Controlled access point is defined as "a name, term, code, etc., under which a bibliographic or authority record or reference will be found" (FRAD 3.4, p. 14). This definition includes both "authorized" or preferred forms as well as variant forms leading—under current authority practice—to the preferred form. This is diagrammed in figure 3.18.

Note that figure 3.18 shows that a controlled access point can be based on more than one name or identifier, but the name, identifier, or name-identifier combination can serve as the basis for only one controlled access point. Similarly, the controlled access point is registered as only one authorized heading or variant heading.

Included are access points based on names or titles of all the FRBR entities and access points based on combinations of names, identifiers, or both. Other pieces of information such as dates that serve to distinguish between entities with identical or similar names can also be part of controlled access points.

Attributes of Controlled Access Point

FRAD assigns thirteen attributes to controlled access point (FRAD 4.14, pp. 26–28), including "type of controlled access point," a categorization such as "personal

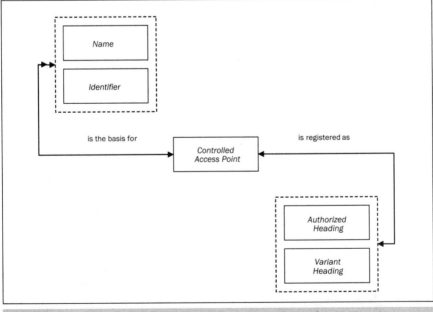

Figure 3.18 Relationship of controlled access point entity to other FRAD entities

name" or "meeting name"; "designated usage of controlled access point," that is, authorized/preferred or variant; "language of base access point," the language in which the base access point is recorded; "base access point," all elements that are integral to the name or identifier that forms the basis of the controlled access point; and "addition," a name, title, date, number, or something else added to the base access point; this is currently referred to as a qualifier and includes fuller forms of names, dates of birth and death for persons, dates of meetings, and the like.

Figures 3.19a and 3.19b diagram two instances of controlled access points, one for the AACR2 authorized ("preferred") heading for Mozart and one for a Japanese variant heading for the same person.

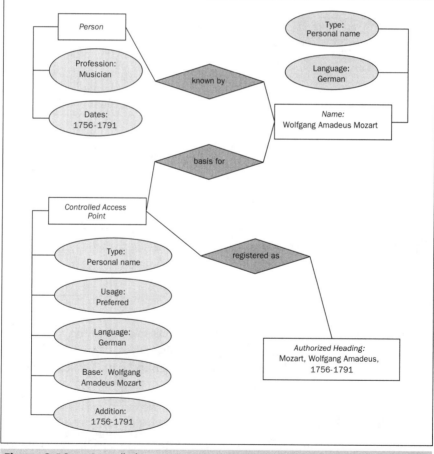

Figure 3.19a Controlled access point (authorized heading)

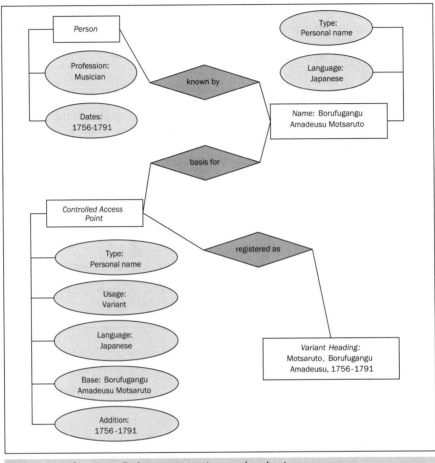

Figure 3.19b   Controlled access point (variant heading)

Rules

The entity *rules* is defined as "a set of instructions relating to the formulation and/or recording of controlled access points" (FRAD 3.4, p. 15). AACR2 is an example of rules. Rules are linked in FRAD to the entity *controlled access point* by a "governed by" relationship, as illustrated in figure 3.20.

Attributes of Rules

Two attributes are defined in FRAD for *rules* (FRAD 4.15, pp. 28–29): "Citation for rules" identifies the cataloging code, instructions, and so forth. Included are

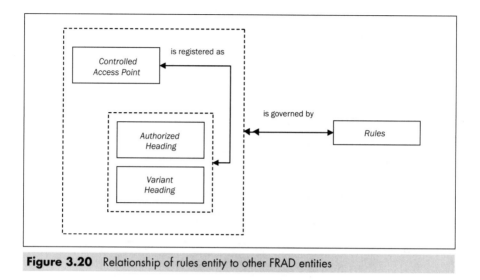

Figure 3.20 Relationship of rules entity to other FRAD entities

the title of the rules and if necessary the body responsible and the edition. This may include a reference to the specific rule being cited. "Rules identifier" is an acronym or code identifying the rules.

Figure 3.21 illustrates the relationship of the entity *rules* to the choice of the controlled access point illustrated in figure 3.19a as the authorized heading. At least three AACR2 rules have a bearing on the formulation of the heading eventually registered as the authorized heading, linked to the entity *controlled access point* by a "governed by" relationship. In the diagram, the dashed lines connect the "rules identifier" attribute of specific rules relating to individual attributes of the controlled access point.

Agency

Agency is the organization responsible for creating or modifying a controlled access point (FRAD 3.4, p. 15). Its relationship in the model to a controlled access point (and also to an authorized heading and variant headings) is "created/modified by." *Agency* also has a relationship to the entity *rules*. Figure 3.22 diagrams these relationships.

Attributes of Agency

Agency has three attributes (FRAD 4.16, p. 29). "Name of agency" is the name by which the agency is commonly known; interestingly, this is the only FRAD entity

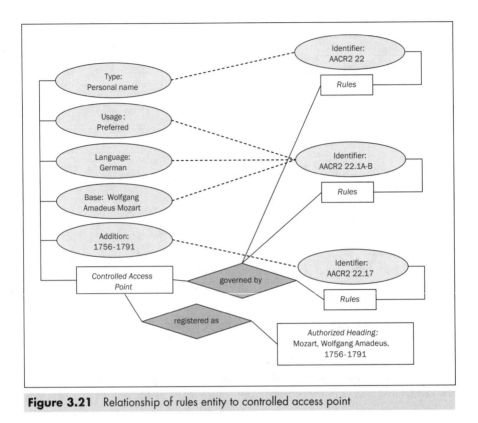

Figure 3.21 Relationship of rules entity to controlled access point

with a "name" attribute. "Agency identifier" is a code identifying the agency, such as the MARC organization code (e.g., DLC is the MARC organization code for the Library of Congress). "Location of agency" is the place where the agency or its headquarters is located.

Agency as an entity has a theoretical problem in the FRAD model, since presumably all agencies are also corporate bodies, a separate FRAD entity.

Undefined FRAD Entities

FRAD does not define several entities that are shown in FRAD figure 5 (p. 63): *uncontrolled access point, authorized heading, variant heading, explanatory heading, authority record, reference record,* and *explanatory record.* All of these entities have to do with current cataloging practice and might not be relevant in an entity-relationship environment.

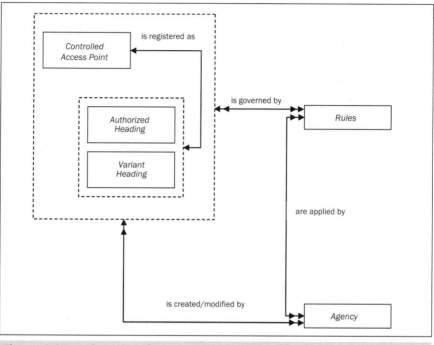

Figure 3.22 Relationship of agency entity to other FRAD entities

Effect of FRBR/FRAD on the Authority Structure of Bibliographic Databases

The idea that an entity with more than one name should be referred to in a bibliographic database by one form only is familiar to most in the library community, although not, perhaps, to most library users. The principal reason it is important to choose a single form is the necessity to record the same form of the name in every bibliographic record in which the name is used so that all instances of the entity collate when a user searches the database. It is not clear that this will be as necessary in an entity-relationship database. In figure 3.17, for instance, the user searching for *The Magic Flute* could initiate a search using that form or the German form *Die Zauberflöte,* each of which is equally linked to the work record by the "known by" relationship. FRAD, on which figure 3.17 is based, does not consider *name* to be an attribute of *work,* and so the name of the work is not even contained in the work record. It is therefore not entirely clear why one form needs to be chosen as the authorized heading and others as variant headings. (It is somewhat clearer in FRBR, where "name" is an attribute of *work* and therefore the work record might contain many instances of the attribute. There might be some reason in that model to choose one as the preferred form.)

It is also not clear whether in a FRBR/FRAD-inspired entity-relationship database there would be any need for authority records. Instead of authority records authorizing forms embedded in bibliographic records, entity-relationship would call for a record for the entity linked by a relationship to another entity. For example, the name of the composer of *The Magic Flute* would not be embedded in the work record or controlled by an authority record. An independent person record would be created for Mozart, linked to name records for the names by which he is known (or following the FRBR model, these names would be recorded as attributes in the person record); this person record would be linked to the work record representing *The Magic Flute* as well as to any other work, expression, manifestation, or item record to which Mozart was related (see figure 3.17).

None of this is to say that FRBR/FRAD would eliminate the need for authority *work*. Much the same process, including adherence to rules and, in some cases, research, would be followed to create a FRBR/FRAD person record, for example, as is now followed to create an AACR2/MARC personal name authority record. It does seem unlikely, however, that a separate authority record would also be required once a person entity record was created in a FRBR/FRAD entity-relationship database.

NOTES

1. See Charles A. Cutter, *Rules for a Dictionary Catalog,* 4th ed. (Washington, DC: Government Printing Office, 1904), 11–12. Cutter's objects have been reprinted many times, including in Michael Carpenter and Elaine Svenonius, eds., *Foundations of Cataloging: A Sourcebook* (Littleton, CO: Libraries Unlimited, 1985), 67.
2. See, for example, Martha M. Yee, "What Is a Work?" in International Conference on the Principles and Future Development of AACR, *The Principles and Future of AACR: Proceedings of the International Conference on the Principles and Future Development of AACR, Toronto, Ontario, Canada, October 23–25, 1997,* edited by Jean Weihs (Ottawa: Canadian Library Association, 1998), 62–104; also available at http://epe.lac-bac.gc.ca/100/200/300/jsc_aacr/whatis/r-whatis.pdf.
3. Richard P. Smiraglia, "Further Reflections on the Nature of 'A Work': An Introduction," *Cataloging and Classification Quarterly* 33, nos. 3–4 (2002): 4.
4. See Smiraglia's summary of discussion by Allyson Carlyle, Martha Yee, and Elaine Svenonius in "Further Reflections," 5–6.
5. IFLA Working Group on the Expression Entity, "FRBR Chapter 3: Entities: Proposed Changes to the FRBR Text," 21 August 2006, p. 2; available at http://www.ifla.org/VII/s13/wgfrbr/FRBR-expression-2006-clean.pdf or http://www.ifla.org/VII/s13/wgfrbr/FRBR-expression-2006-clean.htm.

6. FRAD does define "place of production" as an attribute of the entity *object* (FRAD 4.9, p. 23).
7. Bibliographic Standards Committee, Rare Books and Manuscripts Section, Association of College and Research Libraries, *Descriptive Cataloging of Rare Materials (Books)* (Washington, DC: Cataloging Distribution Service, Library of Congress, 2007), 202. See also John Carter, *ABC for Book Collectors,* 7th ed. (New Castle, DE: Oak Knoll Press, 1995), 100.
8. See *Subject Cataloging Manual: Subject Headings,* 5th ed. (Washington, DC: Library of Congress Cataloging Distribution Service, 1996–2007), section H1631; and *Describing Archives: A Content Standard* (Chicago: Society of American Archivists, 2004), sections 2.6 and 12.29 with chapter 9, as well as the "Bacot Family Papers" example on p. 265.
9. *RDA: Resource Description and Access* will replace AACR2 and is expected to be released in 2009. For more information, see http://www.collectionscanada.ca/jsc/rda.html.
10. For a good summary of problems associated with family names, see Laurence S. Creider, "Family Names and the Cataloger," forthcoming in *Library Resources and Technical Services* 51 (2007).
11. In entity-relationship modeling, the entity name can be split into various subentities, such as first name, last name, alternate name. See, for example, Peter Pin-Shan Chen, "The Entity-Relationship Model: Toward a Unified View of Data," *ACM Transactions on Database Systems* 1, no. 1 (1976): 9–36.
12. Ludwig von Köchel, *Chronologisch-thematisches Verzeichnis sämtlicher Tonwerke Wolfgang Amade Mozarts* (Leipzig: Breitkopf and Härtel, 1862, with later revisions).

CHAPTER **4**

Relationships

Fundamental to an understanding of Functional Requirements for Bibliographic Records is an understanding of bibliographic relationships. FRBR itself devotes an entire chapter to the subject, chapter 5. Relationships are also discussed in FRAD chapter 5.

Bibliographic relationships can exist between any of the FRBR entities. They can exist between independent works, or they can exist between entities within a single work. These are relationships between FRBR Group 1 entities. Bibliographic relationships also exist between the other FRBR entities. For example, creator relationships exist between persons and works, that is, between Group 2 and Group 1 entities. Or relationships exist between works and subjects of works, that is, between Group 1 and Group 3 entities. Relationships also exist within Groups 2 and 3. For example, a relationship exists between a corporate body that has ceased to exist and the corporate body that replaced it; this is a relationship between two Group 2 entities. A relationship exists between a narrow subject term and its immediately broader term; this is a relationship between two Group 3 entities. Relationships also exist between Group 2 and Group 3 entities, though they are rarely brought out in current cataloging. For example, William Shakespeare (a Group 2 entity) is an English author (a Group 3 entity, LCSH "Authors, English"). Although this is not currently done, there is no reason why Shakespeare's authority record could not include a link to the subject term "Authors, English," allowing grouping of English authors within the bibliographic database. This would be a relationship between a FRBR Group 2 and a FRBR Group 3 entity.

Bibliographic relationships have been at the heart of cataloging theory for more than a century. Relationship considerations underlie Cutter's famous objects of the catalog, that the catalog should

1. enable the user to find a book of which either the author, title, or subject is known;
2. show the user what the library has by a given author, on a given subject, or in a given kind of literature; and
3. assist in the choice of a book as to its edition or as to its character.[1]

To accomplish any of these user tasks (to use the FRBR terminology), the user must perform a relationship query of the catalog. To accomplish the first task, the user is looking for a specific resource that shares an author, title, or subject relationship with his or her query—in other words, the user is looking for a relationship between FRBR Groups 2 and 3 entities and FRBR Group 1 entities. To accomplish the second, the user is looking for all resources that share an author, subject, or genre relationship. This, too, requires the catalog to show relationships between all three FRBR groups. To accomplish the third, the user may be examining relationships within a given work, between its various manifestations or expressions, that is, looking for relationships within FRBR Group 1 entities.

Bibliographic relationships between what are now called FRBR Group 1 entities began to be examined seriously in the mid-1980s, when Barbara B. Tillett wrote a dissertation titled "Bibliographic Relationships: Toward a Conceptual Structure of Bibliographic Information Used in Cataloging" (UCLA, 1989). Her findings were summarized in a series of articles in *Library Resources and Technical Services*[2] and have formed the foundation of subsequent research.[3]

Tillett's research resulted in a "taxonomy" of bibliographic relationships. A taxonomy—a term more frequently used with plants and animals than with bibliographic resources—is a classification system showing relationships between the members of the classified group. According to Tillett, "Taxonomic principles require categories to be mutually exclusive and totally exhaustive."[4] This means that each category must be complete in itself and must not overlap with any other category, and that the overall scheme must cover everything within the group being classified. Tillett's taxonomy purports to be such a scheme. She found that the bibliographic universe can be classified into seven different types of relationships:

1. equivalence relationships
2. derivative relationships
3. descriptive relationships
4. whole-part relationships
5. accompanying relationships
6. sequential relationships
7. shared-characteristic relationships

These seven categories have remained standard.[5]

In this chapter, I discuss each of these relationship types, describe how they are brought out in the current AACR2/MARC environment, and show how the same relationship links might be made in a FRBR environment, often more efficiently and more clearly.

Equivalence Relationships

The equivalence relationship is that between a resource and a copy of the resource. There are various types of copies, but in order to have an equivalence relationship, the resources must have the same intellectual or artistic content. The equivalence relationship is that between the various manifestations of an expression of a work (see FRAD 5.3.6, pp. 38–39). In FRBR, this relationship is called a "manifestation-to-manifestation relationship" (FRBR 5.3.4, p. 76).

For example, science fiction author Orson Scott Card's first major work, *Ender's Game,* was first published in 1985 simultaneously in New York by Tom Doherty and in London by Century. These two "editions" have identical text and thus share an equivalence relationship (see figure 4.1).

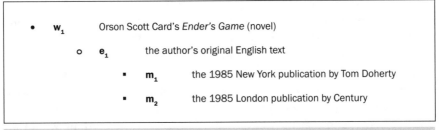

• **w₁**   Orson Scott Card's *Ender's Game* (novel)

    ○ **e₁**   the author's original English text

        ▪ **m₁**   the 1985 New York publication by Tom Doherty

        ▪ **m₂**   the 1985 London publication by Century

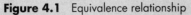

Figure 4.1 Equivalence relationship

As Tillett points out, determination of equivalence can be quite subjective, because different users have different ideas of what is the "same."[6] Most users would probably say that the British and U.S. editions of the first Harry Potter book have an equivalence relationship, considering the differences between American and British spellings and occasional differences in terminology to be irrelevant. Yet the titles between the editions differ—the U.S. edition is *Harry Potter and the Sorcerer's Stone*, the British *Harry Potter and the Philosopher's Stone*. Are the difference of one word in the title and minor variations in the text introduced by the publisher of the U.S. edition enough to remove the two *Harry Potter*s from the relationship category "equivalence"? If so, the relationship would be described as a derivative relationship (see below). In FRBR terms, there are two possible scenarios, illustrated by figures 4.2a and 4.2b.

The choice between these two scenarios is more than simply academic. In a catalog built on FRBR principles, it would make the difference between separating the English and U.S. editions as separate expressions or grouping them all together as manifestations of a single expression. Different communities might make different decisions depending on the needs and wants of their users.

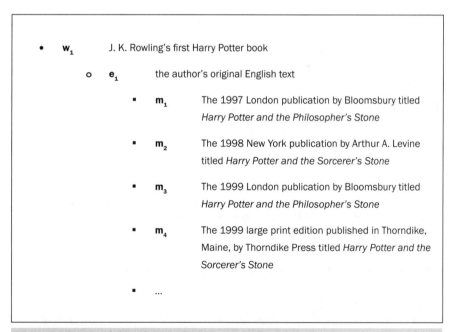

- w_1 J. K. Rowling's first Harry Potter book

  o e_1 the author's original English text

    ▪ m_1 The 1997 London publication by Bloomsbury titled *Harry Potter and the Philosopher's Stone*

    ▪ m_2 The 1998 New York publication by Arthur A. Levine titled *Harry Potter and the Sorcerer's Stone*

    ▪ m_3 The 1999 London publication by Bloomsbury titled *Harry Potter and the Philosopher's Stone*

    ▪ m_4 The 1999 large print edition published in Thorndike, Maine, by Thorndike Press titled *Harry Potter and the Sorcerer's Stone*

    ▪ …

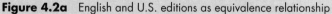

Figure 4.2a English and U.S. editions as equivalence relationship

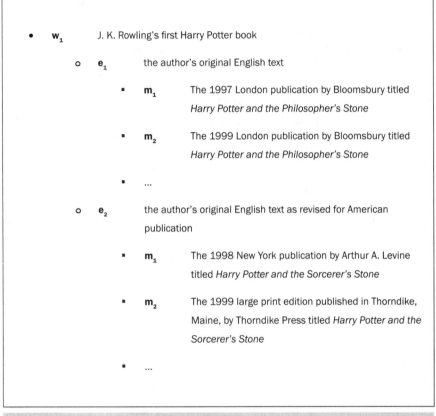

Figure 4.2b   English and U.S. editions as derivative relationship

AACR2/MARC Record

Equivalence relationships are often not explicit in AACR2/MARC records. Determining an equivalence relationship usually requires manual comparison of records. Do the records have the same main entry? The same title? Do they have the same edition statement? Is there a note in one record saying it represents a copy of another resource? Is the physical description the same or similar? (This last clue is only partially relevant, since the same intellectual or artistic content can exist in different physical manifestations.)

A technique showing equivalence relationships used previous to AACR2 was the "dashed-on" entry (see AACR [1967] rules 152–54). Using this technique, the cataloger could signal the existence in a library's collection of, for example, a microfilm copy of a book by adding a "dashed-on" entry to the card at the end of the entry for the book (see figure 4.3a). The notation "— —— Microfilm." indicated that the library owned both the book and a microfilm copy, a resource that had an equivalence relationship with the original.

The "dashed-on" entry technique was eliminated with AACR2, but a sort of grassroots revival of the technique is occurring in some libraries in the treatment of digitized copies of books published on paper. Using a technique called the "single-record technique," catalogers use the same record to direct users to the physical copy and the digital version, sometimes by simply adding a URL to the record for the physical copy. In both the pre-AACR2 "dashed-on" technique and the current "single-record technique," a single record is used to catalog two separate resources that have an equivalence relationship to each other.

FRBR

In a FRBR record set, equivalence relationships, since they appear at the manifestation level, would be shown by linkage of records for manifestations to a single expression-level record. By definition, all manifestations of a single expression have an equivalence relationship with each other. A similar relationship to that illustrated in figure 4.3a (for a microfiche manifestation) could be represented as a FRBR record set using the entity-relationship diagramming in figure 4.3b.

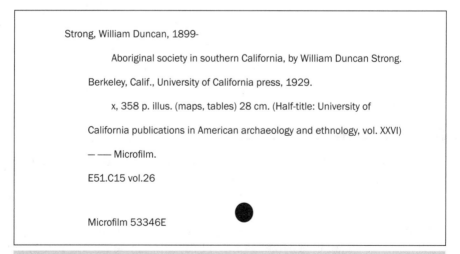

Strong, William Duncan, 1899-

Aboriginal society in southern California, by William Duncan Strong.

Berkeley, Calif., University of California press, 1929.

x, 358 p. illus. (maps, tables) 28 cm. (Half-title: University of

California publications in American archaeology and ethnology, vol. XXVI)

— — Microfilm.

E51.C15 vol.26

Microfilm 53346E

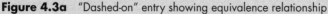

Figure 4.3a "Dashed-on" entry showing equivalence relationship

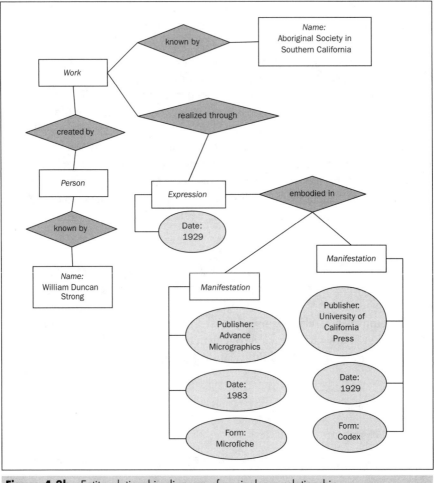

Figure 4.3b   Entity-relationship diagram of equivalence relationship

Derivative Relationships

A derivative relationship is the relationship between a resource and another resource that is based on the first resource, in which the original has been modified in some way. There is, of course, a range of possible modifications, from major to minor (see discussion in FRAD 5.3.6, p. 39). Two resources related by a derivative relationship can be closely enough related that they are considered the same work—for example, a new edition. In FRBR terms, these are schematized as different expressions of the same work (see figure 4.4).

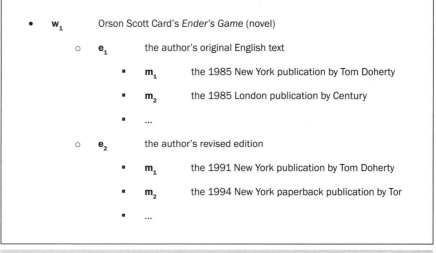

- **w₁**   Orson Scott Card's *Ender's Game* (novel)
  - ○ **e₁**   the author's original English text
    - ■ **m₁**   the 1985 New York publication by Tom Doherty
    - ■ **m₂**   the 1985 London publication by Century
    - ■   ...
  - ○ **e₂**   the author's revised edition
    - ■ **m₁**   the 1991 New York publication by Tom Doherty
    - ■ **m₂**   the 1994 New York paperback publication by Tor
    - ■   ...

Figure 4.4 Derivative relationship (revised edition)

A translation has a derivative relationship with the translated resource. In current thinking, a translation is considered the same work as the original, even though it may share absolutely no text with the original. Thus a translation is a separate expression of the same work as the original (see figure 4.5a).

FRBR has been criticized for needing more refinement at the expression level.[7] The Bulgarian translation of *Ender's Game* was undoubtedly translated from either the author's original English text (**e₁**) or more likely the author's revised edition (**e₂**). But the FRBR schema does not easily allow the translation to be directly linked to the expression it depends on. Rather, it is simply added as an expression at the same level as the English-language expressions. In entity-relationship diagramming, these relationships can be made clear (see figure 4.5b).

The need has therefore been expressed for an intermediate level (and perhaps more than one intermediate level) in FRBR between *expression* and *manifestation* to take care of this problem. On the other hand, in the majority of cases the information needed to take advantage of such intermediate levels will be unavailable. Except for the case of scholarly editions of texts, the resource rarely declares itself to be a derivative resource based on a particular expression. In the case of the Bulgarian translation of *Ender's Game,* there is no way—short of writing the translator and asking—of knowing which edition she based her translation on. So the FRBR schema as currently published represents a practical compromise.

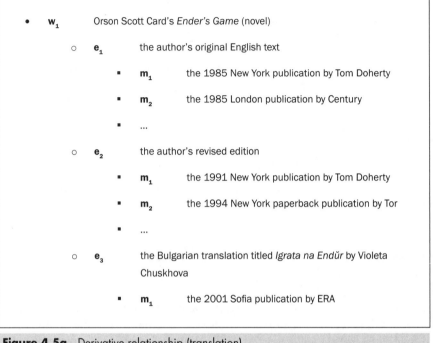

Figure 4.5a Derivative relationship (translation)

Thus far I have discussed derivative relationships between resources that are considered the same work: revised editions and translations. Derivative relationships run the gamut between minor changes to the original and major changes, and at a certain point the changes are considered significant enough that a new work exists. Under current cataloging theory, adaptations and changes of genre are considered "tipping points" where a new work comes into existence instead of a new expression of an existing work.

In 1977, before Orson Scott Card published the novel *Ender's Game*, he published the tale as a short story, also titled "Ender's Game." When he expanded the short story to novel length, he created a new work. The relationship between Card's short story and novel could be diagrammed in FRBR notation as in figure 4.6.

Such relationships can also occur at the expression level (see FRBR 5.3.2, pp. 71–73). In a partial acknowledgment of the need for more refinement at the expression level noted above, the FRBR schema allows for (somewhat clumsy) diagramming of relationships between expressions. For example, the relationship between the Bulgarian translation of *Ender's Game* and the expression on which

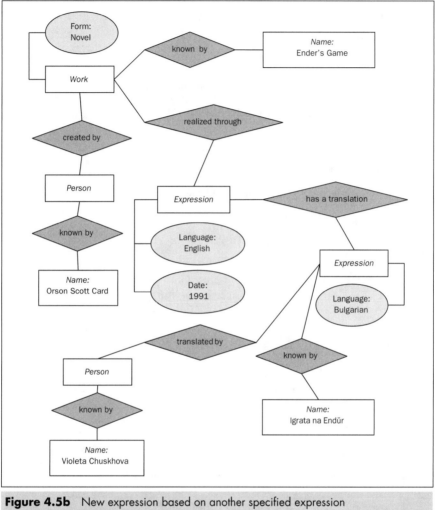

Figure 4.5b New expression based on another specified expression (entity-relationship)

it is based (assuming that can be discovered) could be shown as in figure 4.7, which shows the same relationships as the entity-relationship diagram in 4.5b.

Works that are simply "based on" other works are also said to have a derivative relationship with each other. A game was produced in 2000 based on the first Harry Potter book. It has a derivative relationship with the novel (see figure 4.8).

Films of literary works also share a derivative relationship (see figure 4.9).

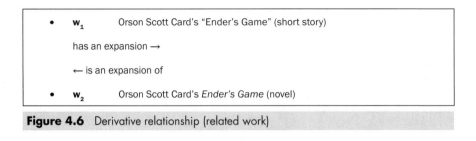

- **w₁**   Orson Scott Card's "Ender's Game" (short story)

  has an expansion →

  ← is an expansion of

- **w₂**   Orson Scott Card's *Ender's Game* (novel)

Figure 4.6 Derivative relationship (related work)

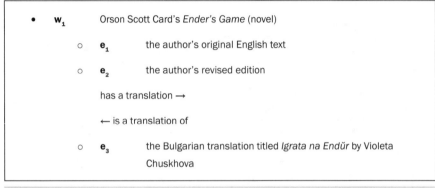

- **w₁**   Orson Scott Card's *Ender's Game* (novel)

  ○ **e₁**   the author's original English text

  ○ **e₂**   the author's revised edition

  has a translation →

  ← is a translation of

  ○ **e₃**   the Bulgarian translation titled *Igrata na Endŭr* by Violeta Chuskhova

Figure 4.7 New expression based on another specified expression (FRBR)

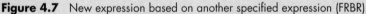

- **w₁**   J. K. Rowling's first Harry Potter book

  is the basis for →

  ← is based on

- **w₂**   "Harry Potter and the Sorcerer's Stone : The Game"

Figure 4.8 Derivative relationship (work based on another)

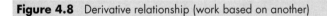

- **w₁**   J. K. Rowling's first Harry Potter book

  has a film version →

  ← is a film based on

- **w₂**   *Harry Potter and the Sorcerer's Stone* (Motion picture)

Figure 4.9 Derivative relationship (film adaptation)

AACR2 recognizes derivative relationships between resources (though it does not so term them) and defines which ones constitute the same work as the original resource and which ones constitute new works (see pp. 17–18). Derivative resources considered in AACR2 to be the same work are represented in the FRBR scheme as different expressions of a single work (see, e.g., figure 4.7). Derivative resources defined in AACR2 as new works are represented in FRBR as separate works related by work-to-work relationships (see, e.g., figure 4.9).

In FRBR, derivative relationships are discussed in several places. They are not called "derivative relationships" in FRBR, but such relationships are found as subcategories of "work-to-work relationships," "expression-to-expression relationships," and "expression-to-work relationships." The following FRBR relationship types are derivative:

Work-to-work relationships (FRBR table 5.1, p. 65); expression-to-expression relationships between expressions of different works (FRBR table 5.4, p. 72); or expression-to-work relationships (FRBR table 5.6, p. 75)

- summarization (some examples of summarization, however, have a descriptive relationship instead)
- adaptation
- transformation
- imitation

Expression-to-expression relationships between expressions of the same work (FRBR table 5.3, p. 71)

- abridgment
- revision
- translation
- arrangement (music)

FRAD discusses derivative relationships at FRAD 5.3.6, pp. 39–40.

AACR2/MARC Record

Resources with derivative relationships to other resources are linked in MARC records by various techniques. A translation is usually linked to its original with a uniform title/work citation:

```
100 1    ‡a Card, Orson Scott.

240 10   ‡a Ender's game. ‡t Bulgarian

245 10   ‡a Igrata na Endŭr ...
```

FRBR

In a FRBR record set, the uniform title/work citation for a translation is either an attribute of the expression-level record (in the FRBR model) or a name entity related to the expression (in the FRAD model).

AACR2/MARC Record

Another (less effective) linking technique is the addition of a note to the record for the translation:

100 1	‡a Card, Orson Scott.
245 10	‡a Igrata na Endŭr ...
500	‡a Translation of: Ender's game.

FRBR

This note describes the expression level and so would be contained in the expression-level record in a FRBR record set.

AACR2/MARC Record

Catalog records for resources with derivative relationships that are sufficiently different to constitute separate works may be linked by a related-work added entry, a note, or both:

130 0	‡a Harry Potter and the sorcerer's stone (Motion picture)
245 10	‡a Harry Potter and the sorcerer's stone ‡h [videorecording] / ‡c directed by Chris Columbus ...
500	‡a Based on the novel by J. K. Rowling.
700 1	‡a Rowling, J. K. ‡t Harry Potter and the philosopher's stone.

The added entry works fairly well to link the original work to the derivative work, although the nature of the relationship is not specified. The note by itself is clearly not a useful linking device.

FRBR

Since the related-work added entry and note describe a relationship between two works, in a FRBR record set the note would be a part of the work-level record for the motion picture, and the AACR2/MARC added entry for the related work would be expressed by a "based on" relationship link between the two work records.

Descriptive Relationships

A descriptive relationship is that between a work and another that describes it, including criticism, evaluations, and reviews. In FRBR terms, this is a relationship between a Group 3 (subject) entity (remember that Group 3 includes all entities in Groups 1 and 2 as well as concepts, objects, events, and places) and a Group 1 entity.

Many works have a descriptive relationship with the film *Gone with the Wind,* including *On the Road to Tara: The Making of Gone with the Wind* by Aljean Harmetz (1996) and *Gone with the Wind on Film: A Complete Reference* by Cynthia Marylee Molt (1990). Their relationship would be diagrammed in FRBR as in figure 4.10a.

Descriptive relationships are not dealt with extensively in FRBR, but subject relationships are dealt with at FRBR 5.2.3, pp. 62–63. A few explicitly descriptive relationships are found in the relationship tables. Certain instances of the relationship type "supplement" could have a descriptive relationship with the related work, although most would instead have an accompanying relationship (see below); and instances of the "summarization" relationship might have a descriptive relationship with the related work, although many would instead have a derivative relationship. These relationship types are found in FRBR tables 5.1 (p. 65), 5.4 (p. 72), and 5.6 (p. 75).

FRAD discusses descriptive relationships at FRAD 5.3.6, p. 40. Because AACR2 does not deal with subject relationships, descriptive relationships are not discussed there.

AACR2/MARC Record

Resources with descriptive relationships to other resources are usually linked in catalog records by subject terms, normally the uniform title or work citation for

> - w$_1$ Gone with the Wind (Motion picture)
>
>   is the subject of →
>
>   ← has a subject
>
>   ○ w$_1$ On the Road to Tara
>
>   ○ w$_2$ Gone with the Wind on Film

Figure 4.10a FRBR diagram of descriptive relationship

the work being described. In a MARC record, the linkage of the records for *On the Road to Tara* and *Gone with the Wind on Film* with the record for the film would consist of the uniform title for the film in a subject field of the records for the books:

630 00   ‡a Gone with the wind (Motion picture)

FRBR

In a FRBR record set, if the descriptive relationship is at the work level, the relationship would be expressed by a "has a subject" relationship link between the work records (see figure 4.10b). If the descriptive relationship is at a different level (e.g., a commentary on a particular edition of the Bible), the relationship link would be between the work-level record (for the commentary) and an expression- or manifestation-level record (for the expression or manifestation described).

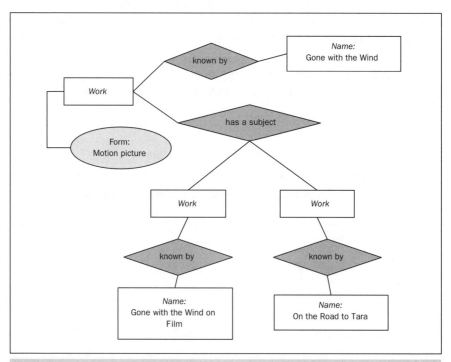

Figure 4.10b   Entity-relationship diagram of descriptive relationship

Whole-Part Relationships

A whole-part relationship is that between a resource and its parts. The relationship includes divisions of what are normally considered single works (e.g., the relationship of a preface or a chapter to the entire work) as well as aggregate works and their parts (e.g., the relationship of a single monograph to its series). FRBR is clear about aggregate entities: for purposes of the model, they are considered works and therefore can have the same relationships as works that exist "primarily as integral units": "The entity *work* may represent an aggregate of individual works brought together by an editor or compiler in the form of an anthology, a set of individual monographs brought together by a publisher to form a series, or a collection of private papers organized by an archive as a single *fond*. By the same token, the entity *work* may represent an intellectually or artistically discrete component of a larger *work*" (FRBR 3.3, p. 28).

Whole-part relationships are discussed in the context of the entity *work* at FRBR 5.3.1.1 with table 5.2 (pp. 69–70), in the context of the entity *expression* at FRBR 5.3.2.1 with table 5.5 (pp. 73–74), in the context of the entity *manifestation* at FRBR 5.3.4.1 with table 5.8 (pp. 77–78), and in the context of the entity *item* at FRBR 5.3.6.1 with table 5.11 (pp. 80–81). FRAD discusses the whole-part relationship in the context of works only, at FRAD 5.3.6, p. 40.

There are several types of whole-part relationships, and they are treated somewhat differently. First, a work that exists primarily as an integral unit (e.g., a novel) is composed of parts, and sometimes it makes sense to treat these parts separately from the work as a whole. For example, the first four books of Homer's epic poem *Odyssey* are often referred to as "The Telemachy" because they concern the adventures of Odysseus's son Telemachus and are considered by some scholars to be a separate work, or at least to be based on a separate work. They are thus sometimes published and studied separately from the work as a whole. "The Telemachy" shares a whole-part relationship with the *Odyssey* and would be represented as in figure 4.11a.

Like any work, a part of a work can exist in many expressions, including translations. "The Telemachy" has been translated into Italian and would be noted as another expression in the schema (see figure 4.11a).

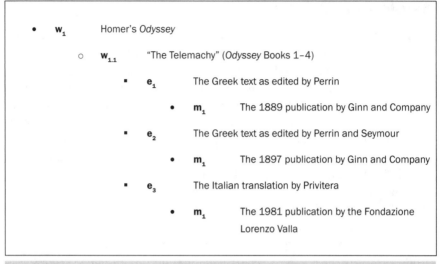

Figure 4.11a Whole-part relationship within a single work

AACR2/MARC Record

Whole-part relationships are usually expressed in MARC records through uniform title/work citation links:

    100 0   ‡a Homer.

    240 10   ‡a Odyssey. ‡p Book 1-4. ‡l Italian & Greek

    245 10   ‡a Odysseia ...

FRBR

Since the part can be considered in FRBR to be a work itself, when treated separately from its "aggregate" work the part would be recorded on a work-level record in a FRBR record set, and links between the two would be at the work level (see figure 4.11b).

Anthology

An anthology has a whole-part relationship between the anthology itself and the individual works within it. For example, T. S. Eliot recorded some of his poems, and these were published in an aggregate work called *T. S. Eliot Reading Poems and Choruses.* Included in this sound recording are eleven separate works. The whole-part relationship is represented as in figure 4.12a.

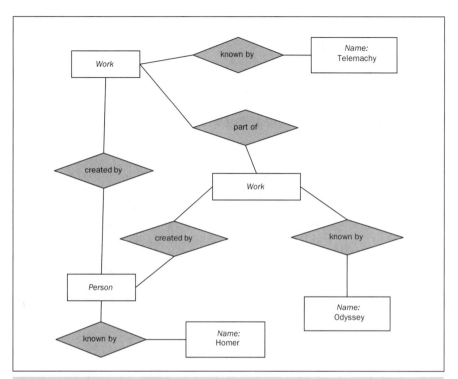

Figure 4.11b Entity-relationship diagram of whole-part relationship (parts of a work)

- **w₁**   *T. S. Eliot Reading Poems and Choruses*

  - ○   **w₁.₁**   "The Love Song of J. Alfred Prufrock"

  - ○   **w₁.₂**   "Portrait of a Lady"

  - ○   **w₁.₃**   "Preludes"

  - ○   **w₁.₄**   "Mr. Eliot's Sunday Morning Service"

  - ○   ...

Figure 4.12a Whole-part relationship (anthology)

AACR2/MARC Record

Linkage between the parts of an anthology and the whole is generally made through a contents note:

> 100 1   ‡a Eliot, T. S. ‡q (Thomas Stearns), ‡d 1888-1965.
>
> 245 10   ‡a T. S. Eliot reading poems and choruses ‡h [sound recording].
>
> ...
>
> 505 0   ‡a The love song of J. Alfred Prufrock -- Portrait of a lady --
>   Preludes -- Mr. Eliot's Sunday morning service -- Ash Wednesday
>   -- A song for Simeon -- Marina -- Triumphal march,
>   from Coriolan -- O light invisible from The rock -- Murder in the
>   cathedral (opening chorus) -- Family reunion (Act II, a chorus).

Stronger links may also be made through analytical added entries:

> 700 12   ‡a Eliot, T. S. ‡q (Thomas Stearns), ‡d 1888-1965. ‡t Love song of
>   J. Alfred Prufrock.
>
> 700 12   ‡a Eliot, T. S. ‡q (Thomas Stearns), ‡d 1888-1965. ‡t Portrait
>   of a lady.
>
> 700 12   ‡a Eliot, T. S. ‡q (Thomas Stearns), ‡d 1888-1965. ‡t Preludes.
>
> ...

In current practice this technique is used only if there are no more than two or three individual works.[8] If used, the field contains the uniform title/work citation for the individual work, not necessarily the title given to it in the anthology.

FRBR

Whole-part linkages within an anthology would be made as an expression-to-work relationship, as in figure 4.12b, which represents the relationship of one of the poems in the anthology illustrated in figure 4.12a to the anthology itself. In this figure the work in the upper left corner is the poem "Portrait of a Lady." This poem was created by a person, T. S. Eliot, who, when he read and recorded the poem, realized an expression of the poem. This recorded poem became a part of another work, the anthology *T. S. Eliot Reading Poems and Choruses,* shown in the lower right-hand corner of the figure. The linkage is from the expression to the work level (rather than expression to expression) because the work (the anthology) consists of a collection of specific expressions; if another anthology were

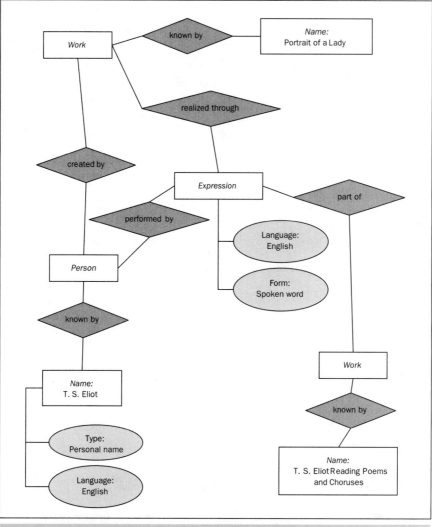

Figure 4.12b   Entity-relationship diagram of whole-part relationship (anthology)

created using different expressions of the same poems, it would be a different work. On the other hand, the same expression of the poem could become part of another anthology (i.e., another work); if so, the link to the other anthology (work) would extend from the same "part of" relationship diamond on the right side of the figure.

Series

The relationship between a series and its parts is a whole-part relationship. The series itself is considered a work in FRBR. Included are multipart monographs and monographic series. For example, the three motion pictures known collectively as the Apu trilogy exhibit a whole-part relationship between the individual works and the trilogy as a whole (see figure 4.13).

A whole-part relationship also exists between the individual monographs in a monographic series and the series itself (which may be numbered or unnumbered) (see figure 4.14a).

AACR2/MARC Record

Two linking techniques are used in MARC records to express the whole-part relationship between individual resources and series they may be a part of. The most common technique is to link records to the series using a controlled series entry:

440   0   ‡a Apu trilogy

or

440   0   ‡a Sather classical lectures

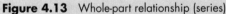

Figure 4.13   Whole-part relationship (series)

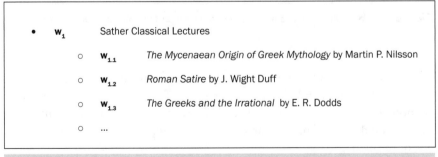

Figure 4.14a   Whole-part relationship (series)

In the case of multipart monographs a second technique is available, linkage via uniform title/work citation:

130 0   ‡a Apu sansār (Motion picture)

245 14   ‡a The world of Apu ‡h [videorecording] = ‡b Apu sansār

Using this technique, the linkage between the whole and the part is made in the authority record for the uniform title/work citation:

130 0   ‡a Apu sansār (Motion picture)

430 0   ‡a Apu trilogy. ‡n 3, ‡p Apu sansār

430 0   ‡a World of Apu

This might display to the user as

Apu trilogy. 3, Apu sansār
        search under
    Apu sansār (Motion picture)

See AACR2 25.6 for further information on this technique.

In current OPACs this is a rather clumsy way to notify the user of the link between the individual work and the aggregate work (the trilogy). Improvements in OPAC displays could give a more FRBR-like display, perhaps leading the user who searched for one of the individual titles to a display something like this:

Apu trilogy
    1. Pather pānchāli
    2. Aparājito
    3. Apu sansār

or perhaps better, taking the user to the requested work but displaying a message such as

For information about other titles in the Apu trilogy, click here.

FRBR

Individual titles within a monographic series or multipart monograph would be linked at the manifestation level with the aggregate work in a FRBR record set. The linkage from the manifestation level for one of the works in figure 4.14a to the work level for its series is shown in figure 4.14b, which also shows the relationship of the expression to a different manifestation. Only one of the manifestations has a relationship with the series.

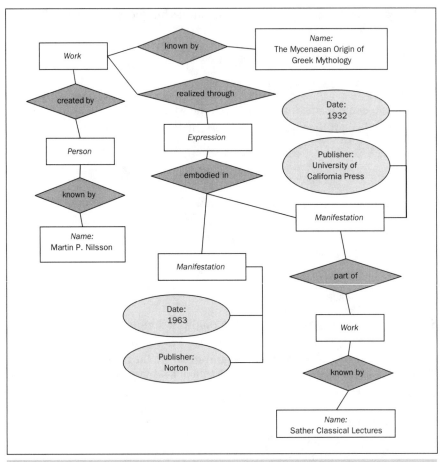

Figure 4.14b Entity-relationships diagram of whole-part relationship (series)

Serial/Monographic Analytics

Individual articles within journals or essays within collections (e.g., in Festschrifts) have a whole-part relationship with the aggregate work (the journal or monograph) (see figures 4.15 and 4.16).

AACR2/MARC Record

There are two techniques used in current cataloging practice to show whole-part links for serial or monographic analytics. The most common method for monographs is the same as for an anthology: a contents note (MARC 505 field), possibly paired with analytical added entries (see the T. S. Eliot example illustrated

Figure 4.15 Whole-part relationship (journal issue)

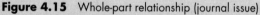

- **w₁**   *The Future of Cataloging: Insights from the Lubetzky Symposium*

    ○ **w₁.₁**   "Introduction" by Robert L. Maxwell

    ○ **w₁.₂**   "Select Bibliography of Publications by Seymour Lubetzky"

    ○ **w₁.₃**   "To Seymour Lubetzky on the Occasion of His First Centennial" by Elaine Svenonius

    ○ **w₁.₄**   "The Vicissitudes of Ideology and Technology in Anglo-American Cataloging since Panizzi and a Prospective Reformation of the Catalog for the Next Century" by Seymour Lubetzky

    ○ ...

Figure 4.16 Whole-part relationship (monograph—Festschrift)

in figure 4.12a). This method works for monographs because they are cataloged on discrete records.

Conversely, individual issues of journals are almost never cataloged on discrete records, so the contents note plus analytical added entries technique would rarely if ever be used to show the whole-part relationship between an issue of a journal and its articles. Traditionally, this relationship is rarely brought out in library catalogs. For very practical reasons it was long ago decided that articles in journals would not usually be given individual entries—or indeed any notice at all—in library catalogs. An analytical technique does exist, however, for the rare cases where individual entries for articles are wanted, described in AACR2 13.5. This technique can be used for articles in monographs or in individual journal issues. When used, the individual work is linked to the aggregate using one of the MARC linking fields, usually 773:

100 1	‡a Johnson, Kij.
245 10	‡a Schrödinger's cathouse / ‡c by Kij Johnson.
300	‡a p. [25]-30 ; ‡c 20 cm.
773 0	‡t The magazine of fantasy & science fiction, ‡g vol. 84, no. 3 (March 1993)

The 773 field produces a note prefaced with "In: . . ." and may also link the record to the "parent" record for the aggregate journal.

FRBR

In a FRBR record set, these linkages would be made from the expression record for the article or story to the work record for the aggregate work (the serial issue or Festschrift) in a similar manner as the anthology illustrated in figure 4.12b. This would allow the user to go seamlessly from the record for the aggregate to the individual subworks. A database designed around FRBR record sets should allow the user to go from the record for the journal itself to records for individual articles (if not to the full text for the articles) whether or not analytical entries have been made for individual articles. FRBRization of our bibliographic databases should allow for seamless melding of catalogs and journal indexes.

Dependent Parts

FRBR makes a distinction between dependent and independent parts (FRBR 5.3.1.1, pp. 67–70). Independent parts do not particularly depend on the larger work for their meaning. For example, the short story "Schrödinger's Cathouse" by Kij Johnson, illustrated in figure 4.15, is an independent part of *Fantasy and Science Fiction* 84, no. 3. If removed from the journal and published somewhere else, it would be just as understandable as it is in its original context.

Conversely, dependent parts are intended to be used in the context of the larger work. Unlike independent parts, dependent parts frequently—usually—do not have distinctive names or titles.

FRBR further divides dependent parts into subcategories: segmental and systematic parts. Segmental parts are identifiable segments of the whole. For example, a chapter in a novel is a segmental part of the novel. Indeed, a single page in a book is a segmental part. In contrast, systematic parts cannot be identified as a sequential segment of the content of a work. Systematic parts extend across the work—in FRBR's words, "interwoven with the rest of the content of the work" (FRBR 5.3.1.1, p. 70). Illustrations added to a text, or background music added to a recording of the spoken word, are examples of systematic parts. They can be discussed and are certainly a part of the intellectual whole, but they cannot easily be quantified as a "section" of the whole.

In traditional cataloging, dependent parts are rarely analyzed on separate records from their work. If an aspect of a dependent part needs to be brought to the attention of the catalog user—for example, the presence of illustrations or a preface by a prominent person—this is typically done by enhancing the record for the larger work, perhaps by creating an added access point for the illustrator or providing a note of some sort.

The FRBR concept of dependent parts, however, becomes crucial when dealing with digital objects. For example, a document containing digitized images of a book may contain a separate file for the image of each page. Each of these discrete files (pages) is a dependent part of the larger work and as such has a whole-part relationship with it. It is absolutely crucial that this relationship is clearly recognized and linked—otherwise the file would be unusable. The user would not be able to go from one page to the next, or find the way to another chapter, if the whole-part relationships within the work were not embedded in the document. The document would simply be a random group of files.

Similarly, in the digital context, though perhaps not as crucial as the whole-part relationship linking the dependent parts (pages) of the document, also extremely useful are whole-part links bringing together groupings of individual images or files into chapters and sections. The linking of whole-part relationships is a part of the structural metadata of the document (which is also called a "compound object"). In electronic journals, recognition and linking of whole-part relationships are what allow an individual issue to have a table of contents through which the user can link to individual articles and then go back to the issue as a whole.

Note that dependent parts are normally an expression-level attribute of the work as a whole. The addition of a preface or illustrations is often what distinguishes one expression from another. Dependent parts can also be manifestation-level attributes. What actually appears on a given page (a dependent part) will likely differ from one manifestation of an expression to another—or the identical text might be published once as a single volume and another time as a five-volume set. Each of these volumes is a dependent part of the whole, and to be usable the parts need to be grouped in some way. But the difference between the single-volume and the five-volume versions are manifestation-level differences. For further information, see FRBR 5.3.2.1, p. 73, and 5.3.4.1, pp. 77–78.

Complexities of Whole-Part Relationships

Thus far we have considered whole-part relationships in the context of a smaller work embedded in a larger aggregate work. But such relationships can become extremely complex, since the smaller work might appear in more than one aggregate work. Consider, for example, the short story "Ender's Game," discussed above in the context of derivative works. "Ender's Game" has been published many times, always with the identical text (i.e., each publication is a separate manifestation of the same expression) (see figure 4.17).

Each of these manifestations has an equivalence relationship to the others and a relationship to the work and to the expression. But they each also have a whole-part relationship with the anthology or journal issue they were published in—each of which is a unique aggregate work. To compare only two, see figure 4.18.

In the bibliographic universe these relationships—and more—exist all at once. It is impossible to diagram them simultaneously in a two-dimensional medium such as ink on paper. Theoretically, however, in a catalog or database founded on FRBR principles, all these relationships could be shown, and individual works, expressions, manifestations, and items could be linked in myriad ways.

- w_1 Orson Scott Card's "Ender's Game" (short story)
  - e_1 The English text of "Ender's Game"
    - m_1 The first publication in *Analog* 97, no. 8 (Aug. 1977), pp. 100–134
    - m_2 Publication in *Analog Readers' Choice*, ed. Stanley Schmidt (New York: Dial, 1981), pp. 254–284
    - m_3 Publication in *There Will Be War*, ed. J. E. Pournelle (New York: TOR, 1983), pp. 73–113
    - m_4 Publication in *Battlefields beyond Tomorrow*, ed. Charles G. Waugh and Martin H. Greenberg (New York: Bonanza Books, 1987), pp. 41–74
    - …

Figure 4.17   Relationship of manifestations of anthologized short story to each other (equivalence)

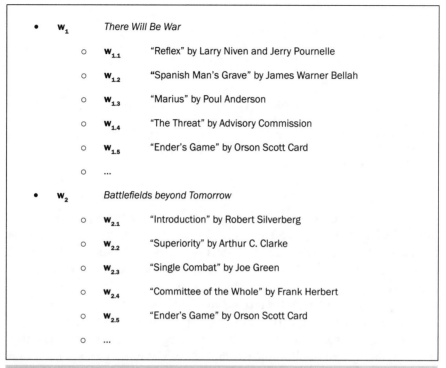

• **w₁**		*There Will Be War*
	○ **w₁.₁**	"Reflex" by Larry Niven and Jerry Pournelle
	○ **w₁.₂**	"Spanish Man's Grave" by James Warner Bellah
	○ **w₁.₃**	"Marius" by Poul Anderson
	○ **w₁.₄**	"The Threat" by Advisory Commission
	○ **w₁.₅**	"Ender's Game" by Orson Scott Card
	○ ...	
• **w₂**		*Battlefields beyond Tomorrow*
	○ **w₂.₁**	"Introduction" by Robert Silverberg
	○ **w₂.₂**	"Superiority" by Arthur C. Clarke
	○ **w₂.₃**	"Single Combat" by Joe Green
	○ **w₂.₄**	"Committee of the Whole" by Frank Herbert
	○ **w₂.₅**	"Ender's Game" by Orson Scott Card
	○ ...	

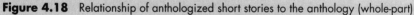

Figure 4.18 Relationship of anthologized short stories to the anthology (whole-part)

Accompanying Relationships

An accompanying relationship is that between an entity and another that accompanies it or is intended to accompany it (see FRAD 5.3.6, p. 41). FRBR tables 5.1 (p. 65), 5.4 (p. 72), and 5.6 (p. 75) include two relationship types that are normally accompanying: supplement and complement.

Supplementary Accompanying Relationships

Accompanying relationships are supplementary when one entity is predominant and the other is subordinate, such as the relationship between a work and its index.[9] Wolfhard Steppe produced an index to James Joyce's *Ulysses* in 1985. Although the novel and the index are widely separated chronologically, they share an accompanying relationship because Steppe's work was intended to accompany Joyce's (see figure 4.19).

- w_1 Joyce's *Ulysses* (1922)

  has an index →

  ← is an index to

- w_2 Steppe's *A Handlist to James Joyce's Ulysses* (1985)

Figure 4.19 Independent supplementary accompanying relationship

In the case of *Ulysses* and its index, the two works are independent of each other. Entities with supplementary accompanying relationships can also be dependent. An index published with a text is an example of such a relationship. Another example is an illustrated text. The text and the illustrations can be considered separate works, each of which has a whole-part relationship with the aggregate work consisting of the text together with the illustrations. As seen above in the discussion of whole-part relationships, these two entities have a systematic, dependent whole-part relationship with the aggregate. In relation to each other, however, the two entities have an accompanying relationship, and in most cases illustrations are considered supplementary to the text, though not always. A well-known example is Lewis Carroll's *Alice's Adventures in Wonderland,* published with illustrations by John Tenniel (see figure 4.20).

Naturally, it is possible to publish illustrations separately from the text, as sometimes happens when the illustrations become particularly famous. For example, Tenniel's illustrations were published without the text as *Tenniel's Alice* (1978). Even though the illustrations were published separately, they still have an accompanying relationship with Carroll's text, since they were intended to accompany it.

It is possible for an entity to have many related supplementary accompanying relationships. *Alice* has been illustrated by many artists over the years (see figure 4.21). All these have an accompanying relationship to *Alice,* and they have a shared characteristic relationship to each other (the shared characteristic being their relationship to the work *Alice*). In an entity-relationship database, their relationship would be expressed by linkages to what they have in common, the text of *Alice.*

Musical works frequently exhibit accompanying relationships. An example that would probably be described as dependent is the relationship of a cadenza

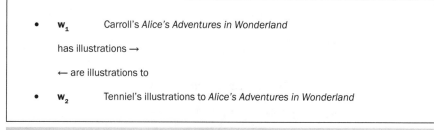

Figure 4.20 Dependent supplementary accompanying relationship

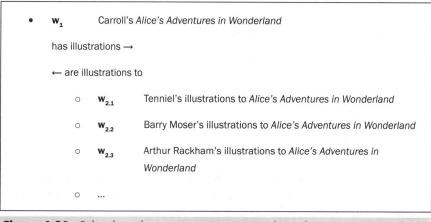

Figure 4.21 Related supplementary accompanying relationships

to a concerto. Composers write concertos to showcase a solo instrument or voice; a typical feature of a concerto is a cadenza in which the soloist performs without accompaniment. Sometimes the cadenza is written as part of the original composition, but the soloist may also be expected to improvise, or the cadenza may be written by a different composer than the composer of the concerto. In this case the cadenza has a dependent accompanying relationship to the concerto (see figure 4.22).

Other examples of supplementary accompanying relationships, any of which may be dependent (published with the primary work) or independent (published separately from the primary work), are guides, appendixes, and supplements.

- w_1 Beethoven's Fourth Piano Concerto

  has a cadenza →

  ← is a cadenza to

  - $w_{2.1}$ cadenza written by Clara Schumann
  - $w_{2.2}$ cadenza written by Johannes Brahms
  - $w_{2.3}$ cadenza written by Arthur Rubinstein
  - ...

Figure 4.22 Supplementary accompanying relationship (cadenza)

Complementary Accompanying Relationships

Accompanying relationships are complementary if entities are of equal status but have no chronological arrangement.[10] Music written for an existing text usually has a complementary accompanying relationship with the text. Individual poems within Shakespeare's plays have frequently had music written for them (indeed, many were intended to be sung). An example is "Sigh No More, Ladies," from *Much Ado about Nothing.* Several composers have written music for this poem, including Peter Sculthorpe (see figure 4.23).

The situation can be reversed. In 1964 the comic team Michael Flanders and Donald Swann wrote words to be sung to the tune of the solo instrument in Mozart's Fourth Horn Concerto (K. 495, movement III) (see figure 4.24).

Relationship of the Accompanying Relationship to the Whole-Part Relationship

Works with accompanying relationships to each other may also have a whole-part relationship with an aggregate work they are a part of. Individual works in an anthology, seen above as having a whole-part relationship to the anthology as a whole, also have a relationship to each other. This relationship is sometimes called a part-to-part relationship. In the Tillett taxonomy these works would be said to have an accompanying relationship to each other, at least within the context of the anthology. In the example given above of anthologies containing the work "Ender's Game" by Orson Scott Card (see figure 4.18), "Ender's Game" has an accompanying relationship to "Reflex" by Larry Niven and Jerry Pournelle in the context of the anthology *There Will Be War* but not in the context of the anthology *Battlefields beyond Tomorrow.*

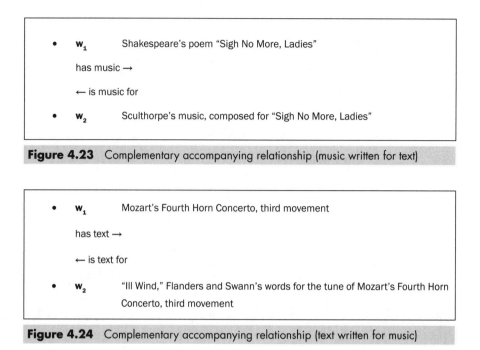

- **w₁**   Shakespeare's poem "Sigh No More, Ladies"

has music →

← is music for

- **w₂**   Sculthorpe's music, composed for "Sigh No More, Ladies"

Figure 4.23 Complementary accompanying relationship (music written for text)

- **w₁**   Mozart's Fourth Horn Concerto, third movement

has text →

← is text for

- **w₂**   "Ill Wind," Flanders and Swann's words for the tune of Mozart's Fourth Horn Concerto, third movement

Figure 4.24 Complementary accompanying relationship (text written for music)

Sequential Relationships

Entities that continue or precede each other, or have a chronological or numerical relationship to each other, are said to have a sequential relationship. The sequential relationship is called a "successor" relationship type in FRBR (tables 5.1, p. 65; 5.4, p. 72; and 5.6, p. 75). It is discussed in FRAD at 5.3.6, p. 41.

Serial

Individual issues of a serial have a sequential relationship to each other. They also have a whole-part relationship to the serial itself (see figure 4.25).

AACR2/MARC Record

The sequential relationship between individual issues of a serial is usually shown in AACR2/MARC cataloging by recording all the issues in a single record, with a numeration field describing the serial as a whole and a holdings record showing the issues owned by the library.

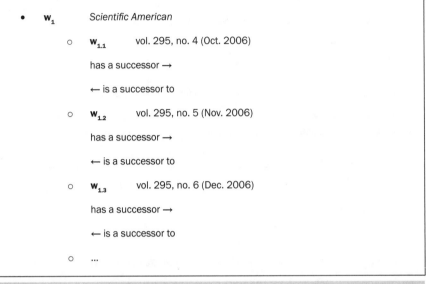

Figure 4.25 Sequential relationship (serial issues)

FRBR

A FRBR record set would presumably describe serials in more or less the same way as an AACR2/MARC record, but a database founded on FRBR principles, particularly when describing an electronic serial, would have the potential of giving links from the serial to individual issues (linking the whole-part relationship) and giving links between one issue and another (linking the sequential relationships).

Sequel

A sequel has a sequential relationship with the work it follows (see figure 4.26a).

AACR2/MARC Record

Sequels and prequels are linked in the AACR2/MARC record by a simple note:

        100 1   ‡a Card, Orson Scott.

        245 10   ‡a Xenocide / ‡c by Orson Scott Card.

        ...

        500   ‡a Sequel to: Speaker for the dead.

        500   ‡a Sequel: Children of the mind.

- **w₁**   The novel *Ender's Game* by Orson Scott Card

    has a successor →

    ← is a successor to

- **w₂**   The novel *Speaker for the Dead* by Orson Scott Card

    has a successor →

    ← is a successor to

- **w₃**   The novel *Xenocide* by Orson Scott Card

    has a successor →

    ← is a successor to

- **w₄**   The novel *Children of the Mind* by Orson Scott Card

Figure 4.26a   Sequential relationship (sequels)

Such informal notes do not allow for very accurate machine detection or display of the sequential relationship.

FRBR

A FRBR record set could have successor linkages at the work level that would allow users to move from one work to another (see figure 4.26b). Such linkage might also allow meaningful index displays such as the following when, for example, a user searches for *Ender's Game:*

> Card, Orson Scott
> > *Ender's game*
> > > sequel: *Speaker for the dead*
> > > sequel: *Xenocide*
> > > sequel: *Children of the mind*

Monographic Series/Multipart Item

Individual works within a numbered monographic series or multipart item usually have a sequential relationship to each other in addition to their whole-part relationship to the aggregate work (see figure 4.27).

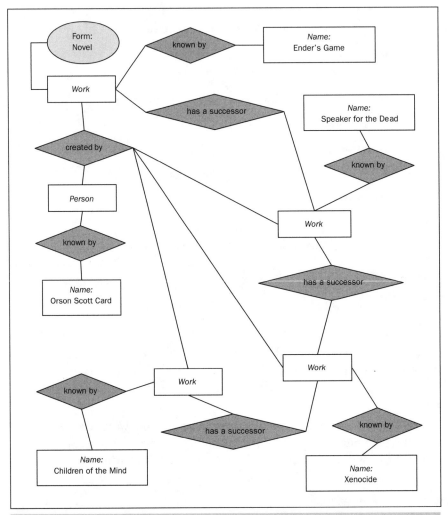

Figure 4.26b Entity-relationship diagram of sequential relationships

AACR2/MARC Record

AACR2/MARC cataloging is fairly successful at showing the sequential relationship between members of numbered monographic series or multipart items. The works are linked by series entries:

- **w₁**   *A Series of Unfortunate Events* by Lemony Snicket

  has parts →

  ← are parts to

  ○   **w₁.₁**   *The Bad Beginning* by Lemony Snicket

  has a successor →

  ← is a successor to

  ○   **w₁.₂**   *The Reptile Room* by Lemony Snicket

  has a successor →

  ← is a successor to

  ○   **w₁.₃**   *The Wide Window* by Lemony Snicket

  has a successor →

  ← is a successor to

  ○   ...

Figure 4.27   Sequential relationship (multipart item)

100 1   ‡a Snicket, Lemony.

245 14   ‡a The bad beginning / ‡c by Lemony Snicket ; illustrations by Brett Helquist.

...

800 1   ‡a Snicket, Lemony. ‡t Series of unfortunate events ; ‡v Bk. 1.

In turn, this field may be indexed in numerical order:

Snicket, Lemony. Series of unfortunate events ; Bk. 1
  The bad beginning
Snicket, Lemony. Series of unfortunate events ; Bk. 2
  The reptile room
Snicket, Lemony. Series of unfortunate events ; Bk. 3
  The wide window

...

This arrangement clearly shows the sequential relationship between the works.

FRBR

As shown in figure 4.14b, the relationship between an individual work in a series and the series itself is a manifestation-to-work relationship. It is therefore likely—since any given expression of one of the works might have manifestations in the series and others not in the series—that in most cases the sequential relationship links between individual titles of a numbered series or multipart monograph would be between manifestation records.

Shared-Characteristic Relationships

Bibliographic resources that do not have one of the above-described relationships but do share a common author, title, subject, or other characteristic are said to have a shared-characteristic relationship with each other. These characteristics might be anything a library user might search for—including date of publication, place of publication, publisher, language, physical characteristics (e.g., a user of a rare book collection might want to find all books with calfskin bindings or printed on vellum), contents (e.g., an art student might want to see all resources with wood engravings), audience (e.g., a teacher might want to find books written for fifth-graders), or combinations (e.g., a language student might want to find books in Afrikaans written within the past ten years for children).

Shared-characteristic relationships are not explicitly mentioned in FRBR as a relationship type, but they are briefly discussed in FRAD, at 5.3.6, p. 42. FRBR does implicitly cover certain shared-characteristic relationships when it discusses how Group 2 entities (persons, corporate bodies, families) are linked to Group 1 entities (works, expressions, manifestations, items) by four relationship types, "created by" (which relates to works), "realized by" (which relates to expressions), "produced by" (which relates to manifestations), and "owned by" (which relates to items) (FRBR 5.2.2, pp. 60–62). FRBR also discusses the "has a subject" relationship between Group 3 and Group 1 entities (FRBR 5.2.3, pp. 62–63).

FRBR presents these as relationships between Group 1 entities and Group 2 or 3 entities, but when database searches are made based on these relationships, the entities found by the search will be related by a shared-characteristic relationship.

"Created by" Relationship

The "created by" relationship is a shared-characteristic relationship in which works are related by the fact that they share a common author. For example, a searcher might look for all the works by Terry Pratchett (see figure 4.28).

Figure 4.28 Shared-characteristic relationship ("created by")

AACR2/MARC Record

AACR2 usually shows the "created by" relationship through the concept of main entry, at least for the primary author, or added entries for other authors. The creator is also usually named in a statement of responsibility. The "created by" relationship is found in a collection of MARC records by performing an author search on a given name. The normal result is a group of manifestation-level records that share a common name in a main or added entry field. Unfortunately, because the nature of the relationship is rarely specified in MARC added entry fields, this search is imprecise and will retrieve more relationships than the "created by" relationship.

FRBR

The FRBR record set would link work-level records to a single record for the creator, resulting in clearer displays and easier moving from one work to the other. Figure 4.26b, for example, shows four separate works linked to a single creator through a "created by" relationship.

"Realized by" Relationship

The "realized by" relationship is a shared-characteristic relationship in which expressions of works (the same work or different works) are related by the fact that they share a common person or body responsible for the realization of the work. There are several different types of "realized by" relationships (e.g., "edited by," "performed by," "illustrated by," "translated by"), and these are used in the diagramming of work-to-expression relationships in this book. For example, a searcher might enjoy an audiobook narrated by Josephine Bailey and be

- p_1 Josephine Bailey
  - e_1 a 1998 reading of Adèle Lang's *Confessions of a Sociopathic Social Climber*
  - e_2 a 2002 reading of Charlotte Brontë's *Jane Eyre*
  - e_3 a 2003 reading of Frances Hodgson Burnett's *The Secret Garden*
  - ...

Figure 4.29a Shared-characteristic relationship ("realized by")

interested in hearing others. A database founded on FRBR principles should allow the user to find the person entity "Josephine Bailey" and then all the expression entities related by the "performed by" relationship to "Josephine Bailey" (see figure 4.29a).

AACR2/MARC Record

In AACR2/MARC records, persons who have a "realized by" relationship to an expression of a work may be recorded in a performance note and are normally given an added access point to the record, so that a user of the database searching for the work of a particular performer would perform an "author" search in the catalog, getting a result of a group of manifestation-level records, as in the creator search. In current practice the exact nature of the relationship (e.g., "edited by," "performed by") is not usually specified.

FRBR

The FRBR record set would link expression-level records to a record for the person or body responsible for the realization of the expression or expressions (see figure 4.29b). This would potentially result in a clearer display of results to the user and allow for easier navigation between records.

"Produced by" Relationship

The "produced by" relationship is a shared-characteristic relationship in which manifestation-level entities (these can be of the same work/expression or of different works) are related by the fact that they share a person or body responsible for the production of the work. The producing entity can be, among other

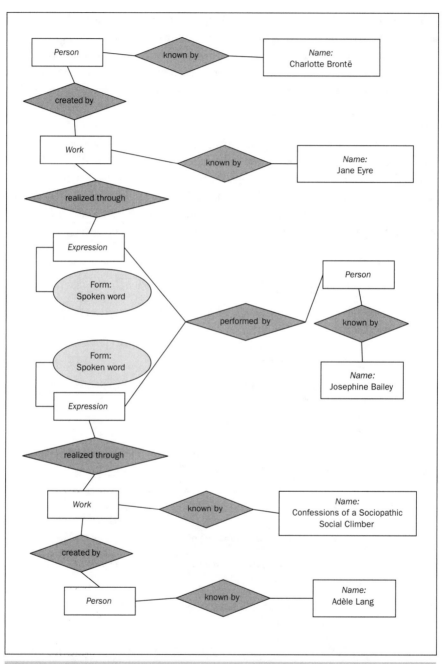

Figure 4.29b Shared-characteristic relationship ("performed by")

things, a publisher, a distributor, or a manufacturer (e.g., printer). For example, a researcher working on a biography of the famous arts and crafts figure Elbert Hubbard would likely want to examine the books he printed at his Roycroft Shop (see figure 4.30). Since these were all also produced by the Roycroft Shop, the same manifestations could be represented in relation to this body (see figure 4.31).

AACR2/MARC Record

AACR2/MARC cataloging does not bring out this relationship very well. Publishers are normally recorded in the publication information field (260) but not in a uniform way. This makes retrieval difficult. Producers and manufacturers (e.g., printers) are in general cataloging normally not recorded at all. In specialist cataloging, such as rare book cataloging, printers (e.g., Elbert Hubbard and the Roycroft Shop) are usually, though not always, given an added entry, a controlled

---

- p_1 Elbert Hubbard
  - m_1 The 1898 publication of *The Rubaiyat of Omar Khayyam*
  - m_2 The 1898 publication of *Sermons from a Philistine Pulpit* by William McIntosh
  - m_3 The 1898 publication of *Confessions of an Opium-Eater* by Thomas De Quincey
  - ...

Figure 4.30   Shared-characteristic relationship ("produced by")

- cb_1 Roycroft Shop
  - m_1 The 1898 publication of *The Rubaiyat of Omar Khayyam*
  - m_2 The 1898 publication of *Sermons from a Philistine Pulpit* by William McIntosh
  - m_3 The 1898 publication of *Confessions of an Opium-Eater* by Thomas De Quincey
  - ...

Figure 4.31   Shared-characteristic relationship ("produced by")

form that allows access. This controlled form may have a relator term or code added to specify the function of the name:

      700 1   ‡a Hubbard, Elbert, ‡d 1856-1915, ‡e printer. [relator term]

or

      700 1   ‡a Hubbard, Elbert, ‡d 1856-1915. ‡4 prt [relator code]

Without a relator term or code—which is not mandatory in current cataloging practice—it is impossible for a system and sometimes difficult for a human to determine the function of the entity named in the added entry. Is Elbert Hubbard cited because he printed the book? Because he illustrated it? Because he edited it?

FRBR

A FRBR record set would likely handle this relationship better than the current MARC structure, making links between the person or corporate body entity and manifestation-level records for which the person or body had a "produced by" responsibility. But whether the records actually contain such links will depend on the cataloging rules and practices in effect when such record sets come into existence. If FRBR record sets are housed in an entity-relationship database, it seems possible that all entities might be linked in such a way, but this is unknown.

"Owned by" Relationship

The "owned by" relationship is a shared-characteristic relationship in which item-level entities are related by the fact that they have a common owner (see figure 4.32). This relationship is particularly important when a user is searching a shared database in which many entities contribute their holdings. To obtain the wanted item, the user must discover who the owner associated with a given record is.

AACR2/MARC Records

AACR2 has little to contribute to bringing out the "owned by" relationship, since AACR2 cataloging for the most part is concerned with manifestation-level records. In a given library's MARC database, the "owned by" relationship is generally manifested by the fact that an item is in the database and has a call number or other method that allows the library user access to it. In a shared database the "owned by" relationship is shown by codes linking a given library's records to records for a particular manifestation, or by coding that identifies a particular record as belonging to a particular library.

- **cb$_1$**   Brigham Young University Library

  - **i$_1$**   a copy of the 1985 New York publication of *Ender's Game* by Orson Scott Card

  - **i$_2$**   a copy of the 1997 London publication of *Harry Potter and the Philosopher's Stone* by J. K. Rowling

  - **i$_3$**   a copy of the 1896 Kelmscott Press publication of *The Works of Geoffrey Chaucer*

  - ...

Figure 4.32   Shared-characteristic relationship ("owned by")

- **c$_1$**   Motion picture music

  is the subject of →

  ← has a subject

  - **w$_1$**   Ian Johnson's *William Alwyn: The Art of Film Music*

  - **w$_2$**   Matthew Caley's *Pop Fiction: The Song in Cinema*

  - **w$_3$**   Pauline Reay's *Music in Film: Soundtracks and Synergy*

  - ...

Figure 4.33   Shared-characteristic relationship (subject)

FRBR

In a FRBR record set the "owned by" relationship could be manifested by a link between an item-level record and a record for the owning entity.

Subject Relationship

Subject relationships are shared-characteristic relationships in which otherwise unrelated entities are related by the fact that they have a common subject. FRBR calls this a "has as subject" relationship (FRBR 5.2.3, pp. 62–63). This relationship allows the user to identify by subject all relevant works in a given collection and to select those most suited to his or her needs (see figure 4.33).

AACR2/MARC Record

AACR2 does not deal with subject relationships. In the MARC record, linkage between entities sharing a subject relationship is made by subject strings in 6XX fields. Since subject analysis is by definition subjective, meaning different catalogers might apply different subject terms to the same item, this is a difficult relationship to bring out consistently.

FRBR

The subject entity (remember that any FRBR entity can serve as a subject) is normally related to the work entity, so in a FRBR record set subject linkages would usually be made in a work-level record (for an example, see figure 4.10b). The same caveat about subject analysis will no doubt apply in a FRBR environment as applies to cataloging in a MARC environment, that is, different catalogers might arrive at different subject analyses of the same work. One advantage of recording subject linkages at the work level would be consistency within a single work. In the MARC environment, where records in the database are usually cataloged at the manifestation level, the same subject strings need to be added to each record for a given work—and they often are not, through neglect or lack of time to compare records when cataloging a given manifestation. This problem presumably would not exist in the FRBR environment; most subject analysis or linkage would be done once at the work level and not repeated in lower-level records.

Not all subject analysis is appropriate to the work level, however. For example, it is customary to add a subject string of the type "Homer—Translations into English" to the record for a translation, such as the *Odyssey* in English. This subject string is not appropriate to the work *Odyssey* itself, which was not a translation, so it would be inappropriate in a FRBR work-level record. Rather, it would appropriately be recorded in the expression-level record for a given translation of the *Odyssey* into English.

Similar examples could be given for manifestation-level subject analysis. If genre/form is considered a kind of subject analysis, this would frequently be recorded at the manifestation level. For instance, in special collections cataloging genre/form terms are often added to records for various physical characteristics or other aspects of the manifestation, such as "Woodcuts" for a book containing woodcuts. Since these apply to a particular manifestation, in a FRBR environment they would be recorded at the manifestation level. Some may even be at the item level (e.g., an early book with a unique binding might have a form term such as "Vellum bindings" applied at the item level).

Sample FRBR Record Set

Relationships in a FRBR record set might be diagrammed as in figures 4.34a–d.

In figure 4.34a, note that the expression record e_1 is linked at the same hierarchical level as the other entities (p_1, c_1, c_2), all linked to work record w_1. This same entity e_1 appears near the top of figure 4.34b.

In figure 4.34b, note that the manifestation records m_1 and m_2 are linked at the same hierarchical level as entities p_2 and c_3, all linked to expression record e_1. These same entities m_1 and m_2 also appear in figure 4.34c.[11]

In figure 4.34c, note that the item record i_1 is linked at the same hierarchical level as entities cb_2, cb_3, and c_4, all linked to manifestation record m_2. This same entity i_1 also appears in figure 4.34d.

In the diagram worked out in figures 4.34a–d, each bulleted line is a separate entity. In a database founded on FRBR principles, each entity would have only one record associated with it, linked to as many other entities as necessary. For example, Alexander Pope's name would not need to be repeated in each record for a manifestation associated with him (as is now the practice). Rather, one record would be created for him and linked to as many work, expression, or other entity records as he has bibliographic relationships.

Each arrow in the diagrams represents a link with a higher or lower entity in the hierarchy. The words associated with the arrows designate the type of relationship represented by the link. In a database founded on FRBR principles, it should be possible for the user to discover all instances of the entity "Alexander Pope" where he is linked by a "translated by" relationship to another FRBR entity, or all instances of the entity "Joh. Enschedé en Zonen" where it is linked by a "printed by" relationship. Indeed, the system should enable the user to find all instances of a relationship—such as "translated by" or "printed by"— without reference to a specific Group 2 entity, in order to see all entities that are represented as linked by a particular relationship type in the database.

Figures 4.35a–e (beginning on p. 118) show this same information using entity-relationship diagramming, which brings out the FRBR record sets more graphically than the FRBR diagramming.

- **w₁**   *The Iliad*

  has an author →

  ← is the author of

  - **p₁**   Homer

  has a subject →

  ← is the subject of

  - **c₁**   Trojan War—Poetry

  has a genre →

  ← is the genre of

  - **c₂**   Epic poetry

  has an expression →

  ← is an expression of

  - **e₁**   an English translation of *The Iliad*

Figure 4.34a   Work record and its links

- **w₁**   *The Iliad*

  has an expression →

  ← is an expression of

  - **e₁**   an English translation of *The Iliad*

    has a translator →

    ← is the translator of

    - **p₂**   Alexander Pope

    has a genre →

    ← is the genre of

    - **c₃**   Epic poetry, Greek—Translations into English

    has a manifestation →

    ← is a manifestation of

    - **m₁**   an electronic version of the text published in 2006
    - **m₂**   a text-on-paper version published in New York in 1931

Figure 4.34b   Expression record and its links

    ○   **e_1**   an English translation of *The Iliad*

has a manifestation →

← is a manifestation of

    ■ **m_1**   an electronic version of the text published in 2006

has a publisher →

← is the publisher of

        ● **cb_1**   ebooks@Adelaide

has an editor →

← is the editor of

        ● **p_3**   Steve Thomas

    ■ **m_2**   a text-on-paper version published in New York in 1931

has a publisher →

← is the publisher of

        ● **cb_2**   Limited Editions Club

has a printer →

← is the printer of

        ● **cb_3**   Joh. Enschedé en Zonen

has a typeface [a genre/form concept] →

← is the typeface of

        ● **c_4**   Romanée type

has an item →

← is an item of

        ● **i_1**   a copy in the Harold B. Lee Library

Figure 4.34c   Manifestation record and its links

- **m$_2$**   a text-on-paper version published in New York in 1931

has an item →

← is an item of

  - **i$_1$**   a copy in the Harold B. Lee Library

  has an owner →

  ← is the owner of

    - **cb$_4$**   Harold B. Lee Library

  has a signer →

  ← is the signer of

    - **p$_4$**   Jean van Krimpen [the designer of the book]

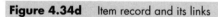

Figure 4.34d   Item record and its links

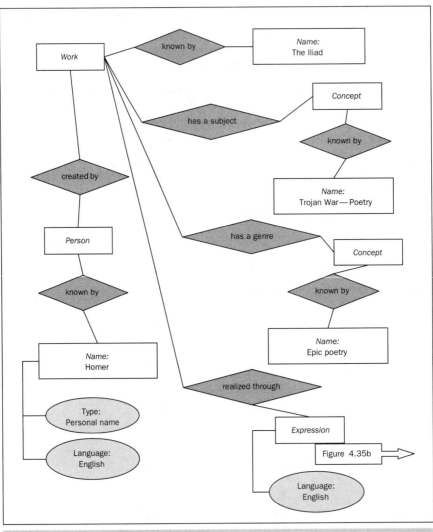

Figure 4.35a Figures 4.34a–d as an entity-relationship diagram

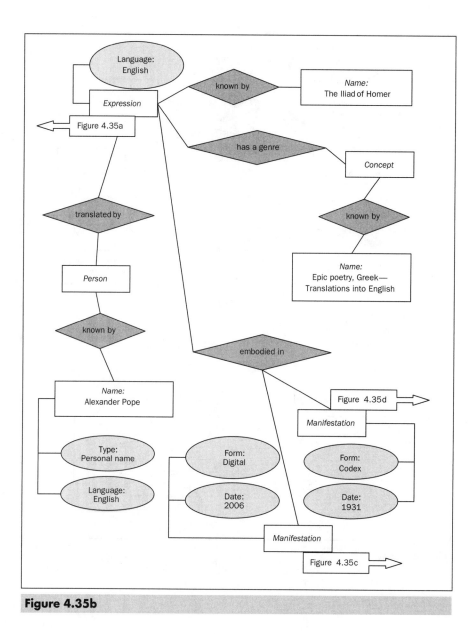

Figure 4.35b

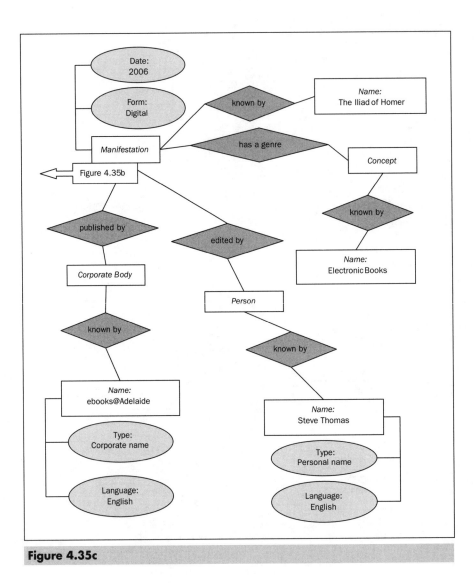

Figure 4.35c

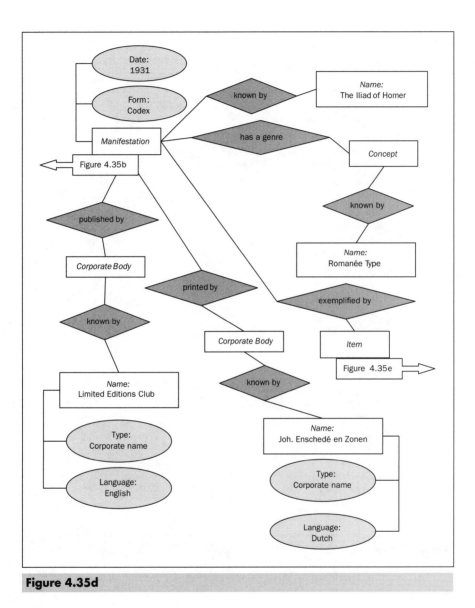

Figure 4.35d

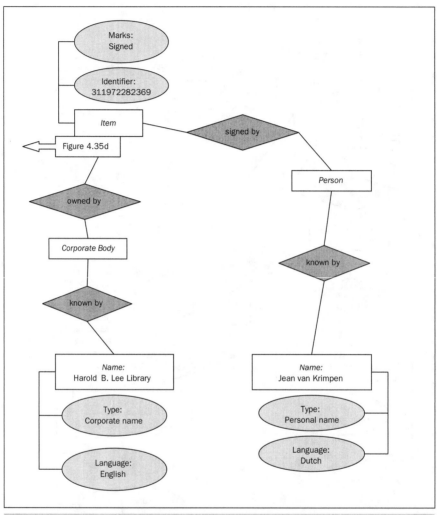

Figure 4.35e

NOTES

1. See Charles A. Cutter, *Rules for a Dictionary Catalog*, 4th ed. (Washington, DC: Government Printing Office, 1904), 11–12. Cutter's objects have been reprinted many times, including in Michael Carpenter and Elaine Svenonius, eds., *Foundations of Cataloging: A Sourcebook* (Littleton, CO: Libraries Unlimited, 1985), 67.
2. Barbara B. Tillett, "A Taxonomy of Bibliographic Relationships," *Library Resources and Technical Services* 35, no. 2 (1991): 150–58; "A Summary of the Treatment of Bibliographic Relationships in Cataloging Rules," *Library Resources and Technical Services* 35, no. 4 (1991): 393–405; "The History of Linking Devices," *Library Resources and Technical Services* 36, no. 1 (1992): 23–36; "Bibliographic Relationships: An Empirical Study of the LC Machine-Readable Records," *Library Resources and Technical Services* 36, no. 2 (1992): 162–88.
3. For example, Sherry Vellucci, "Bibliographic Relationships," in International Conference on the Principles and Future Development of AACR, *The Principles and Future of AACR: Proceedings of the International Conference on the Principles and Future Development of AACR, Toronto, Ontario, Canada, October 23–25, 1997*, edited by Jean Weihs (Ottawa: Canadian Library Association, 1998), 105–46; also available at http://epe.lac-bac.gc.ca/100/200/300/jsc_aacr/bib_rel/r-bibrel.pdf and http://epe.lac-bac.gc.ca/100/200/300/jsc_aacr/bib_rel2/r-bib.pdf [bibliography].
4. Tillett, "Taxonomy," 153.
5. See Vellucci, "Bibliographic Relationships," and Barbara B. Tillett, "Bibliographic Relationships," in *Relationships in the Organization of Knowledge*, edited by Carol A. Bean and Rebecca Green (Dordrecht: Kluwer Academic Publishers, 2001), 19–35.
6. Tillett, "Bibliographic Relationships" (2001), 24; see also FRAD 5.3.6, p. 39.
7. For example, Associazione italiana biblioteche, "Osservazioni su Functional Requirements for Bibliographic Records, Final Report = An Italian Comment on Functional Requirements for Bibliographic Records, Final Report," in *FRBR Seminar: Functional Requirements for Bibliographic Records = Requisiti funzionali per record bibliografici: Florence, 27th–28th January 2000*, edited by Mauro Guerrini (Rome: Associazione italiana biblioteche, 2000), 151–60.
8. See AACR2 21.7B. Practice for sound recordings is to make analytical added entries for up to fifteen works (LCRI 21.7B).
9. See Tillett, "Bibliographic Relationships" (2001), 20.
10. See ibid. Entities with a chronological arrangement are said to have a sequential relationship to each other.
11. Entity $\mathbf{m}_1$ may be accessed at http://etext.library.adelaide.edu.au/h/homer/h8ip/, viewed May 1, 2007.

5

The User Tasks

The main purpose of the FRBR study was to find out which parts of bibliographic records are most helpful in aiding users to achieve their goals. Users are defined in FRBR quite broadly and encompass traditional library users (including library staff) as well as publishers, retailers, and providers and consumers of information outside the library (see FRBR 1.2, p. 4). Why do users do research in bibliographic databases? The authors of FRBR concluded that there are four basic reasons, which they call "user tasks":

1. Users need to *find* materials relevant to their needs. They may be looking for a specific resource (e.g., a score of Lowell Liebermann's piccolo concerto or a recording of James Galway's performance of that concerto), or they may not have a specific resource in mind (e.g., a piccolo player interested in expanding her repertoire might be interested in finding all recordings and scores of piccolo music the library owns or has access to).

2. Users need to *identify* the resource retrieved during the finding process, that is, they must confirm that the resource corresponds to what they were looking for. For example, if our piccoloist looking for the Liebermann

concerto searched for "piccolo concerto" in the database, she would need to confirm by examining the resulting record(s) that one of them represents the Liebermann concerto and not that of Antonio Vivaldi, Martin Amlin, or Peter Maxwell Davies. On the other hand, if the user searched for "Lowell Liebermann," perhaps adding "concerto," she would need to confirm by examining the records that one of them represents the piccolo concerto and not the trumpet concerto or the flute concerto.

3. Users need to *select* a resource appropriate to their needs. If the piccoloist has found and identified recordings of the Galway performance in three formats, she needs to select the one that corresponds to the playback equipment she has (e.g., audiocassette, compact disc, MP3). Or a user of the collection searching for a copy of the *Odyssey* whose search retrieves expressions in French, English, Italian, Russian, and Greek needs to be able to select among these, choosing one in a language he understands. Or a user of an online bookseller's bibliographic database might appreciate the opportunity to select between hardcover and paperback versions of the resource.

4. Finally, once a user has selected a resource, he or she needs to *obtain* it. This might mean the record informs the user where on the shelf the item is, or it might direct the user to interlibrary loan, or in the case of digital objects it might provide a link directly to the resource. In any case, it is unlikely that the average user approaches a catalog or other database just for the pleasure of "surfing"—users have a goal in mind and want to leave the database having obtained a resource at the end of the process. (Note that in some cases "obtain" might, however, include simply obtaining information, as when a user approaches a catalog or database to compile a bibliography without necessarily intending to get the resources themselves.)

The FRBR study group assessed the value of each of the attributes of the so-called primary entities (*work, expression, manifestation, item*) and each of the relationships to those entities in the context of the four user tasks. In an elaborate set of charts (the tables in FRBR chapter 6), each attribute or relationship is assigned one of four values: highly important, moderately important, of low importance, or of no importance.

The assignment of values to attributes of entities and to relationships is clearly a fairly subjective activity. The authors of FRBR acknowledge this by stating that their assessment is based "in large part on the knowledge and experience of the study group members and consultants, supplemented by evidence in the library science literature gathered from empirical research" (FRBR 1.2, p. 5), though this research is not cited. Further, the FRBR study was undertaken to determine the functional requirements for bibliographic records in national bibliographic databases, that is, the most general bibliographic databases. This is reflected in the value assessments for the entity attributes and relationships. Specific attributes or relationships might be found to be more or less important to the user tasks in other types of databases, such as that of a medical library or a rare books collection. The variety of different types of bibliographic databases needs to be kept in mind while examining the assessed values found in the charts in FRBR chapter 6.

Rather than examine those charts in detail, it might be more useful to consider how users behave when they are trying to accomplish the four user tasks. What do they actually do when interacting with a bibliographic database?[1]

Finding and Selecting a Work

The first task is to *find*. What does a user typically do to find a work? Let us say I want to read Oscar Wilde's *The Picture of Dorian Gray*. My first impulse is to type the title of the work into the search box of the database. This is consistent with the FRBR study group's assessment: the only attribute of a work assessed to be of high value for the user task of finding a work is the attribute "title of the work" (FRBR table 6.1, p. 88).

This work, of course, has a relationship with a person, the author Oscar Wilde. I thus might instead approach the catalog hoping to find the work via the author's name, especially if I could not remember the title (perhaps just remembering "that book by Wilde about the guy whose painting grows old while he remains young"). The relationship between a work and the person responsible for it is given a high value in table 6.1 (FRBR, p. 89).

Perhaps I cannot even remember the name of the author, just the subject. Although this might be tricky given the rules and syntax of current subject analysis, as a library user I should be able to find a work via its relationship with a concept entity, such as "portraits" or "old age" or "youth," possibly combined with a genre concept such as "fiction" to limit the set of results. Recognizing this, table 6.1 attributes high value to the relationship between a work and an entity treated as the subject of the work (FRBR, p. 89).

Once I have done a bibliographic database search and received a set of results, my next task is to *identify*. When I search my own library catalog for "picture of dorian gray," my general keyword search returns fifty items. But these are not all the work *The Picture of Dorian Gray* by Oscar Wilde. Many are works *about* the book. Some are other works with the same name (e.g., film versions, or an opera by Lowell Liebermann). My task is to identify which of these correspond to what I actually want, the novel. How do I do this?

One approach is to look through the index screen for hits that have the exact title: *The Picture of Dorian Gray*. This would rule out works with titles such as *A Synthesis of Dance and Drama: Creating a Stage Adaptation of The Picture of Dorian Gray Utilizing Choreography and Dramatic Dialogue*. This scanning method is a bit awkward, but a quick look at my resulting set reveals several editions of the novel that I could choose from. Relevance ranking would probably improve this, but even without it I found what I wanted fairly easily. What I have done is identify the work's record by verifying that the title is the same. "Title of the work" is ranked of high value in table 6.1 for the user task of identifying a work.

A second approach to identifying that I use as I scan the screen of results for the search "picture of dorian gray" is to check to see which records have the correct author, Oscar Wilde. This is easy enough in this case, since the main entry of a record appears on the index screen of my library catalog. As expected, in FRBR the relationship between a work and the person responsible for the work is ranked of high value in identifying a work (FRBR table 6.1, p. 81).

At this point I might get smart and redo my search, asking the database to retrieve records that have both the title *The Picture of Dorian Gray* and the author Oscar Wilde. This brings the result set down to a more manageable number consisting mainly of expressions of the work I am interested in.

Identifying and Selecting an Expression

In the preceding discussion I started my search just wanting a copy of *The Picture of Dorian Gray* to read. But suppose I am in an English literature class and am directed to have a look at the introduction to a publication of the novel edited by Donald Lawler. My task now is to find and identify this expression of the work. Most likely I will follow many of the same steps as above, but this time I would refine my search by adding Lawler's name. I am identifying the particular expression via the name of a person "responsible for content," a relationship identified in FRBR table 6.2 as of high value to identifying an expression.

In the absence of such a requirement, I am back to my original result set. I have identified a group of expressions, all expressions of the work *The Picture of Dorian Gray* by Oscar Wilde. I do not care to identify a specific expression. But now my task is to *select* the expression that meets my need. Perhaps I am interested in an audiobook because I am about to take a long road trip. I will select the expression by its form. In the database I am searching, several of the hits display the term "sound recording." This helps me select the expression I want. I further need a copy on compact disc because that is the type of player in my car. I have refined my search by the form of the item and found an expression that meets my needs. "Form of expression" is ranked of high value to the user task "select an expression" in FRBR table 6.2, p. 91.

Suppose, on the other hand, I am learning German and want to read a copy of the work in an expression in that language. In that case, of overriding importance in the selection process is that the expression be in German. Instead of selecting the compact disc, I will select the expression titled *Das Bildnis des Dorian Gray*. "Language of expression" is ranked of high value to the user task (FRBR table 6.2, p. 91).

If I am away from the library and accessing its collections remotely, I want an online digital expression. If I am given the choice between two such expressions, but the record for one indicates that I can access it only from machines within the library building, or only if I am a member of a particular group (say a student in a particular English class), I will not select that expression. "Use restrictions on the expression" is another important attribute of the expression entity for the selection user task, ranked of high value (FRBR table 6.2, p. 91).

Identifying and Selecting a Manifestation

Back in my English literature class, perhaps my professor referred me to the Lawler edition of the work by telling me to consult the Norton Critical Edition of *The Picture of Dorian Gray* rather than referring to it by Lawler's name. Norton Critical Edition is a series, one of the attributes of manifestation. I would use this in my search (or scanning of a hit list) to identify and select the manifestation I wanted. "Series statement" is rated in table 6.3 (FRBR, p. 93) as of high value for identification of the manifestation and of moderate value in selection.

Perhaps I am writing a research paper for this class on the publication history of *The Picture of Dorian Gray*. I need to see a few specific manifestations of this work, namely, the first few editions. How will I approach the task of identifying these particular manifestations? I learn from the Lawler Norton Critical Edition that the work was first published in *Lippincott's Monthly Magazine* in July 1890, and a second expression, revised with additional chapters, was copublished the next year by Lippincott (Philadelphia) and Ward, Lock and Co. (London), who also happened to be the publishers of *Lippincott's Monthly*. This expression became the basis for most subsequent manifestations. How will I find these first two editions? I will most likely look for records containing the publisher's name (Lippincott or Ward, Lock and Co.), or look for records with publication date 1890 or 1891, or both. I am thus identifying the manifestation by the name of the publisher and the date of publication, both attributes rated of high value for identification of a manifestation (FRBR table 6.3, p. 93). Date is also ranked of high value for selection of a manifestation, perhaps on the assumption that most users, when given a choice between two expressions, would likely want to see the latest expression. In the scenario described here, this assumption is not true. Publisher is rated as of only moderate value for selection of a manifestation, perhaps because all other things being equal it is unlikely that a user would choose between manifestations solely on the basis of the publisher, though again in certain cases it might be a factor.

Obtaining an Item

FRBR is written as though it is possible to *obtain* a manifestation, but what the user actually wants to obtain is a single instance of a manifestation, that is, an item. As discussed in chapter 3, *manifestation* is an abstract concept, and one cannot obtain an entire manifestation; even if it were possible to acquire every copy of an entire print run one would not "have" a manifestation, one would simply have a set of items. So in this discussion I concentrate on obtaining an item, not a manifestation.

What are the attributes of *item* that are of highest value for obtaining an item? Clearly I want to know where to get it and if it is available to me. In my search for the Norton Critical Edition of *The Picture of Dorian Gray*, I was informed by the catalog that it was available on the "Library Bookshelves" at call number PR 5819 .A1 1988, which allowed me to go down to the shelves and retrieve it. Call number is an item identifier, assessed by the FRBR Study Group as of high value in obtaining an item (FRBR table 6.4, p. 96).

In the more general "dorian gray" search, I found that the library had access to remote-access digital versions. To "obtain" one of these I need to know its URL, which functions very like a call number for an ink-on-paper book—it tells where it "resides." The URL is another sort of item identifier, and one that is crucial to allowing the user to obtain this item.

"Access restrictions" is another attribute of an item that is of high value for completing the user task of obtaining an item (FRBR table 6.4, p. 96). As a user I need to know if there are any restrictions on my use of the item, or indeed if I can get it at all. With the digital versions of *Dorian Gray,* for example, the records all state that "access may be limited to . . . affiliated libraries." If I am in the library building itself, I will probably be able to access the item, but if I am away— perhaps accessing the catalog record from home—I will undoubtedly have to authenticate myself in some way to prove that I am affiliated with the library in order to be allowed to see the item. If I was not affiliated with the library and one of the three records allowed me to see the item without any such restriction, that is the item I would select.

Another type of access restriction is availability of the book. When I executed my general search on "picture of dorian gray," one of the resulting records, for a 1998 manifestation, displayed the message "All copies currently checked out or unavailable," and I was given the option to place a hold on the title. The fact that the book has been checked out is certainly a type of access restriction, one that will prevent me from obtaining the book quickly and that will probably cause me to select another manifestation if one is available. Similar access restriction messages might include messages like "Not yet cataloged—ask at a reference desk," which allows the user to request expedited cataloging, or "No copies yet available. Copies on order," informing the user that the book is not yet in the library. All of these will be impediments to the user in obtaining the item.

A third kind of access restriction came up during my search. The first and second expressions, which I need for my paper about the publication history of the novel, are shown in the catalog to be in Special Collections. Although not explicitly spelled out in the catalog record, this entails an access restriction: I will be able to use the books only in the Special Collections reading room, under supervision and during the hours Special Collections is open. If these restrictions do not appeal to me, I might have to reconsider my paper topic.

FRAD User Tasks

FRAD has a distinct set of user tasks from FRBR, which is natural since FRAD deals with a different sort of data, authority data (see FRAD chapter 6, pp. 50–55). FRAD defines the term *user* more narrowly than FRBR. For FRAD, there are two kinds of users of authority data: (1) those who create and maintain authority files and (2) those who use authority information indirectly through messages displayed or links in library catalogs or other databases or who use it directly through access to authority files. According to FRAD, these users have the following user tasks: *find, identify, contextualize,* and *justify.*

Find is similar to the FRBR user task of the same name. The user needs to find an entity corresponding to stated criteria (including attributes and relationships).

Find also includes, according to FRAD, the activity of "explor[ing] the universe of bibliographic entities using . . . attributes and relationships."

Identify, as in FRBR, means to confirm that the entity found corresponds to the entity sought. The activity includes distinguishing between entities with similar or identical characteristics. *Identify,* for a cataloger, also includes the activity of validating the form of a name he or she wants to use as a controlled access point in a catalog record.

Contextualize means to place an entity into context. It includes clarifying relationships between entities or between names. This user task is presumably undertaken only by the first set of users, creators of authority data, but the resulting contextualization is useful to all users in the *identify* user task.

Justify means to document one's reasons for choosing a name or term on which a controlled access point is based. Like *contextualize, justify* is a user task undertaken only by creators of authority data.

Like FRBR, FRAD analyzes the values of various entities and attribute or relationship combinations, but it does not attempt relative valuing. The charts in FRAD table 4 (pp. 51–55) simply state that an attribute or relationship is of value or of no value.

Suppose, to illustrate the user tasks, that I am cataloging a recording of the Liebermann piccolo concerto discussed above. Because I do not intend to create authority data, I have two tasks: to find and identify the appropriate authority data. As a user of the data, my first reaction is to find the form by typing in the person's name. But how do I know the name? The name appears in the title of the CD: *James Galway Plays Lowell Liebermann.* Given all the evidence I have, this person is "known by" the name "Lowell Liebermann." So that is the name I will use as I try to find authority data about him. Thus it is not surprising that the "known by" relationship between the entities *person* and *name* is cited as of value to the user attempting to find something.

Using this name, I search the authority file and find only one record corresponding to this name, with the form "Liebermann, Lowell." This authority record is accompanied by a large set of music uniform title records based on the form "Liebermann, Lowell." Before I even look at the base authority record, from the index display of this set of authority records I know that the authority record set most likely deals with a composer. I next examine the authority record for the base heading, "Liebermann, Lowell." In it I see two notes, one informing me that this person composed "Concerto for piano and orchestra (1983)" and another, citing a work called *American Keyboard Artists,* revealing that his full name is Lowell Seth Liebermann, that he was born in 1961, and that he is a pianist, composer, and conductor. I am able to conclude from all this evidence that this authority record represents the person who composed the piccolo concerto on the CD I am cataloging. I have identified the entity, completing the second user task.

The note from *American Keyboard Artists* contains information about Liebermann's "field of activity," one of the FRAD attributes of *person*. "Field of activity" is also implied in the title of the CD, as well as by the presence of the authority record in a cluster of authority records for music uniform titles. "Field of activity" is shown in FRAD table 4 as an attribute of value in accomplishing identification tasks. I also might have used the attributes "dates of person"— perhaps the CD booklet gave Liebermann's birth date, information also found in the authority record—to link the name on my CD to the entity represented by the authority record. This attribute is also listed as of value for identification.

Now suppose I found nothing in the authority file for this person. As a cataloger, my task would be to create authority data for the entity. My attempt to find and identify met with failure because the information was not there. But I still have two user tasks, to contextualize and to justify.

When I create the authority record, I will include one or more notes citing information I find. I will at least cite the title of the manifestation I am cataloging:

    670   ‡a James Galway plays Lowell Liebermann, p1988

This note contextualizes the name in a few ways. First, from the title it is clear that Liebermann is a composer. A later user of the data who knows who James Galway is might assume that Liebermann composed for flute, since that is Galway's chief instrument. This is a fairly minimal amount of contextualization. If I have done some research, I might add other notes citing more information. Perhaps, like the cataloger who created the authority record that in fact exists, I check the source *American Keyboard Artists*. I would report my research as follows:

    670   ‡a American keyboard artists, 1992: ‡b (Liebermann, Lowell Seth;
               b. Feb. 22, 1961; pianist, composer, conductor)

The addition of details further contextualizes the name. I have accomplished the needed contextualization, chiefly by adding information about Liebermann's field of activity and date of birth. Oddly, however, these attributes are not listed in FRAD table 4 as of value to the task of contextualizing.

As a creator of authority data I also need to justify, that is, document my reasons for choosing the name "Lowell Liebermann" as the basis for a controlled access point. Since the cataloging rules instruct me to choose the form found on chief sources of information if the person is a composer (AACR2 22.1A, 22.1B, and LCRI 22.1B), I document my choice by transcribing the title as in the first "670" note given above. Since the form "Lowell Liebermann" is found in the title, I have documented my reasons for choosing the name. I have completed the justification by citing a "known by" relationship between the name and the person.

NOTE

1. A good discussion of the user tasks is found in a paper presented at the CILIP Umbrella Conference, Manchester, England, July 3–5, 2003, by Tom Delsy, published as "Functional Requirements for Bibliographic Records: User Tasks and Cataloguing Data: Part 1," *Catalogue and Index* 150 (Winter 2003): 1–4, and "Functional Requirements for Bibliographic Records: User Tasks and Cataloguing Data: Part 2," *Catalogue and Index* 151 (Spring 2004): 1–4. This paper is one of the few publications to examine FRBR user tasks in detail.

CHAPTER 6

The FRBR Model and the Existing MARC and AACR2-Based Cataloging Model

FRBR makes no recommendation as to actual database structure for cataloging (see FRBR 1.2, p. 3), but given the entity-relationship structure of the FRBR model the logical next step would be to adopt an entity-relationship database structure, a radical departure from our current MARC databases.

MARC was originally designed as a flat-file system, with all information about a book or other format item stored within a single bibliographic record divided into fields of fixed or variable widths. As the system evolved, the authorities format was added, allowing possible relational aspects to the database structure, but the bibliographic format record continues to contain aspects of all the FRBR entities in flat-file style.

Particularly problematic is the difficulty of extracting and separating the four Group 1 entities from the single MARC bibliographic record. Various pieces of the MARC bibliographic record apply to *work, expression, manifestation,* and sometimes *item,* but it has been found to be quite difficult to define explicitly that a certain field or subfield applies to a particular FRBR Group 1 entity, though some progress has been made.[1]

A particular problem has been the identification in large databases such as OCLC of bibliographic records that are instances of the same work or the same expression. In the absence of an explicit work or expression identifier, automated matching algorithms have difficulty linking, for example, manifestations of a single expression that have different titles. Being able to do this accurately—split the MARC record into work, expression, manifestation, and item records and then link multiple manifestation records to the correct expression record and multiple expression records to the correct work record—is essential, however, for transforming a MARC flat-file database into a FRBR entity-relationship database. This may require a fair amount of manual work, a daunting task in an environment of tens of millions of MARC records.[2] Still, research at OCLC has revealed that an estimated 80 percent of all published works exist in only a single expression and manifestation—in other words, have been published only once. Only 20 percent of works exist in two or more manifestations.[3] This shrinks the pool of records requiring manipulation considerably; of the 20 percent of works existing in two or more manifestations, a large percentage of them could be split using automated algorithms such as that developed at OCLC; a smaller percentage would require some sort of intervention.[4] Of the remaining 80 percent, the single MARC bibliographic record represents the only instance of the work, expression, and manifestation and could be split into its respective FRBR Group 1 entities without the necessity of linking other manifestations to the expression or other expressions to the work.

Thus there will be difficulty converting our MARC bibliographic databases with respect to the FRBR Group 1 entities. Group 1 entities are not, however, the only FRBR entities found in MARC records. All the entities in Groups 2 and 3—for example, *person, corporate body, concept*—are also found in MARC bibliographic records and will need to be split off into separate entity records. These FRBR entities exist as clearly defined pieces of the MARC record. For example, a name found in a 110, 610, or 710 field is for a FRBR corporate body entity. FRBR Group 2 and 3 entities also correspond quite closely to the name and subject authority records formulated under the MARC authorities format. Many of the attributes defined in FRBR and FRAD for these entities are already being recorded in the authority records. The ever-growing set of authority records could easily serve as a transition to FRBR Group 2 and 3 entity records. Although in many applications each authorized form is repeated within individual MARC bibliographic records, the authority record could become the basis of an entity record in an entity-relationship database. Some MARC-based systems already do this, having all the information about an entity (person, corporate body, concept, etc.) contained in the authority record, with a simple link to the authority record at the appropriate spot in the MARC bibliographic record (although for convenience to the user, the heading usually appears in the display of the MARC bibliographic record).

The most fundamental problem for using our set of authority records as a basis for FRBR entity records is the fact that not all headings used in bibliographic records have had authority records made, for one reason or another. Still, the existing set is a good start.

Although splitting the MARC bibliographic record into work, expression, manifestation, and item entity records has proved to be difficult, here too the authority records may help. Authority records for uniform titles might serve as the basis for expression or manifestation records (see discussion of the relationship of uniform titles to works, expressions, and manifestations in chapter 3). The problem of matching bibliographic records lacking uniform title headings to the appropriate work, expression, or manifestation record that might be created in this way will, however, remain a challenge.

So much for the FRBR entities in MARC databases. But splitting the records into entities is only a small part of the task. As we have seen in the preceding chapters, relationships are equally important in an entity-relationship database. In such a database it is important to know that there is some sort of relationship present between entities, but it is crucial to know the nature of that relationship. For example, is the nature of the relationship between a person and an expression that of author (e.g., producer of a revised edition)? translator? editor?

If our MARC bibliographic records are difficult to split into works, expressions, manifestations, and items, the nature of the relationships between the headings on those records (consisting chiefly of Group 2 and 3 entities) and the manifestations described in the MARC records will be even more difficult to tease out. Cataloging rules have long provided for the addition of designation of functions to headings for persons, such as "ill." (illustrator), "ed." (editor), "tr." (translator), and "comp." (compiler), which might have served as an aid to identifying the nature of the relationship (see ALA Cataloging Rules for Author and Title Entries 157A and AACR2 21.0D1). This addition was, however, made optional in AACR2, and the Library of Congress promptly by LCRI instructed its catalogers not to apply the option. This LCRI was followed by most North American catalogers and remains in effect to this day despite criticism.[5] Furthermore, such terms were never applied in the rules to corporate body headings (although it is common practice so to apply them among the group of catalogers that continue to use relator terms in spite of the LCRI).

In the absence of such a term (or code) in a MARC bibliographic record, automated identification of the nature of the relationship will in many cases be impossible. Likely an assumption could be made that names appearing in the main entry position (1XX) have an authorial or creator relationship with a work (although that assumption cannot apply to pre-AACR2 records), but no such assumption can be made for names appearing in the added entry position (7XX), which will exhibit a wide variety of relationships to the work, expression, manifestation, or item.

When FRBR burst on the scene in 1998, it generated a great deal of excitement, but little apparent movement toward conversion of our cataloging databases to an entity-relationship model has been made in the intervening decade, although FRBR continues to inspire a great deal of discussion and experimentation.[6] Also surprising is the fact that many metadata models, including databases incorporating Dublin Core, appear not to take advantage of FRBR entity-relationship models. It is probable that the lack of progress, at least in the traditional MARC-based cataloging arena, is due to the huge inertia imposed on the process by our enormous files of legacy data, which continue to be added to at an ever-increasing rate. It is estimated that a new record is added to OCLC's WorldCat database every ten seconds.[7] Every added record is another record that might need conversion and splitting into entities and relationships in the future if we ever make the transition to entity-relationship. It might be a useful strategy at some point simply to declare a new beginning and start building shared bibliographic databases on the FRBR entity-relationship model, leaving the legacy data to be converted and added to the new databases as time and resources allow.

Splitting our MARC bibliographic records into FRBR entities and relationships is a daunting task and will undoubtedly occupy organizers of information for some time. The advantages of transforming our databases into entity-relationship databases modeled on FRBR are clear, however, and the work involved will be effort well spent, particularly in a period when the search capabilities of our catalogs are increasingly under fire. The implementation of FRBR and FRAD should be an important part of a suite of changes to improve access to information in our libraries.

NOTES

1. See, for example, Rick Bennett, Brian F. Lavoie, and Edward T. O'Neill, "The Concept of a Work in WorldCat: An Application of FRBR," *Library Collections, Acquisitions and Technical Services* 27, no. 1 (2003): 45–59, also available at http://www.oclc.org/research/publications/archive/2003/lavoie_frbr.pdf; and Thomas B. Hickey and Edward T. O'Neill, "FRBRizing OCLC's WorldCat," in *Functional Requirements for Bibliographic Records (FRBR): Hype or Cure-All?* edited by Patrick Le Boeuf (New York: Haworth Information Press, 2005), 239–51, also published as *Cataloging and Classification Quarterly* 39, nos. 3–4 (2005): 239–51.
2. The OCLC WorldCat database reached one hundred million bibliographic records in March 2007. These shared records represent over a billion holdings in individual

libraries. See http://www.oclc.org/worldcat/database/default.htm for a description of OCLC WorldCat.

3. Bennett, Lavoie, and O'Neill, "Concept of a Work," 57.

4. See Hickey and O'Neill, "FRBRizing," for a description of the OCLC algorithm; see also the Library of Congress's "FRBR Display Tool" developed by the Network Development and MARC Standards Office, available at http://www.loc.gov/marc/marc-functional-analysis/tool.html.

5. See, for example, Barbara B. Tillett, *What Is FRBR? A Conceptual Model for the Bibliographic Universe* (Washington, DC: Library of Congress Cataloging Distribution Service, 2004), 3: "The value of this 'role' information becomes very apparent in light of FRBR. We need to regain the lost link of relator terms and codes in our bibliographic records. It is time to re-examine a change in cataloging practice that abandoned the use of 'relator' terms and codes to cut cataloging costs. In hindsight we can see that decision was unfortunate for future users of our records and should be reversed to allow greater flexibility in manipulating bibliographic data and offering better information to users as they navigate our catalogs."

6. For a discussion of some important FRBR implementation experiments, see Brad Eden, "FRBR Implementations," *Library Technology Reports* 42, no. 6 (2006): 32–41. Most of the implementations examined are available on the Internet.

7. See http://www.oclc.org/worldcat/statistics/default.asp, accessed May 5, 2007. This web page has a link to a "Watch WorldCat Grow" feature that dramatically allows the user to see new records as they are added to the database.

SUGGESTED READINGS

Basic Documents

FRBR Review Group (Patrick Le Boeuf, editor; Pat Riva, Review Group Chair). *FRBR Bibliography.* Kept up-to-date and available at http://www.ifla.org/VII/s13/wgfrbr/bibliography.htm.

IFLA Study Group on the Functional Requirements for Bibliographic Records. *Functional Requirements for Bibliographic Records, Final Report.* UBCIM Publications, New Series, vol. 19. München: K. G. Saur, 1998. Also available at http://www.ifla.org/VII/s13/frbr/frbr.pdf or http://www.ifla.org/VII/s13/frbr/frbr.htm.

IFLA Working Group on Functional Requirements and Numbering of Authority Records (FRANAR). *Functional Requirements for Authority Data: A Conceptual Model.* Draft 2007-04-01. Available at http://www.ifla.org/VII/d4/FRANAR-ConceptualModel-2ndReview.pdf.

Secondary Literature

In addition to the following, readers who are interested in keeping abreast of developments in FRBR should subscribe to the FRBR Review Group's discussion list. Subscription information can be found at http://www.ifla.org/VII/s13/wgfrbr/listserv.htm. Additionally, a FRBR blog is being maintained at http://www.frbr.org by William Denton, who regularly posts information about new publications, projects, or experiments.

Associazione italiana biblioteche. Gruppo di studio sulla catalogazione. "Osservazioni su Functional Requirements for Bibliographic Records, Final Report = An Italian Comment on Functional Requirements for Bibliographic Records, Final Report." In *FRBR Seminar: Functional Requirements for Bibliographic Records = Requisiti funzionali per record bibliografici: Florence, 27th–28th January 2000,* edited by Mauro Guerrini, 151–60. Rome: Associazione italiana biblioteche, 2000.

Chen, Peter Pin-Shan. "The Entity-Relationship Model: Toward a Unified View of Data." *ACM Transactions on Database Systems* 1, no. 1 (1976): 9–36.

Hickey, Thomas B., and Edward T. O'Neill. "FRBRizing OCLC's WorldCat." In *Functional Requirements for Bibliographic Records (FRBR): Hype or Cure-All?* edited by Patrick Le Boeuf, 239–51. New York: Haworth Information Press, 2005. Also published as *Cataloging and Classification Quarterly* 39, nos. 3–4 (2005): 239–51.

Le Boeuf, Patrick. "Brave New FRBR World." Prepared for the 4th IFLA Meeting of Experts on an International Cataloguing Code (IME ICC 4), August 16–18, 2006, Seoul, South Korea. Paper available at http://www.nl.go.kr/icc/paper/2-1.pdf; PowerPoint handout at http://www.nl.go.kr/icc/paper/2-3-1.pdf.

———. "FRBR and Further." *Cataloging and Classification Quarterly* 32, no. 4 (2001): 15–52.

———. "FRBR: Hype or Cure-All?" In *Functional Requirements for Bibliographic Records (FRBR): Hype or Cure-All?* edited by Patrick Le Boeuf, 1–13. New York: Haworth Information Press, 2005. Also published as *Cataloging and Classification Quarterly* 39, nos. 3–4 (2005): 1–13.

Madison, Olivia M. A. "The Origins of the IFLA Study on Functional Requirements for Bibliographic Records." In *Functional Requirements for Bibliographic Records (FRBR): Hype or Cure-All?* edited by Patrick Le Boeuf,

15–37. New York: Haworth Information Press, 2005. Also published as *Cataloging and Classification Quarterly* 39, nos. 3–4 (2005): 15–37.

Patton, Glenn E. "Extending FRBR to Authorities." In *Functional Requirements for Bibliographic Records (FRBR): Hype or Cure-All?* edited by Patrick Le Boeuf, 39–48. New York: Haworth Information Press, 2005. Also published as *Cataloging and Classification Quarterly* 39, nos. 3–4 (2005): 39–48.

Tillett, Barbara B. "Bibliographic Relationships." In *Relationships in the Organization of Knowledge,* edited by Carol A. Bean and Rebecca Green, 19–35. Dordrecht: Kluwer Academic Publishers, 2001.

———. *What Is FRBR? A Conceptual Model for the Bibliographic Universe.* Washington, DC: Library of Congress Cataloging Distribution Service, 2004. Also available at http://www.loc.gov/cds/downloads/FRBR.pdf.

INDEX

Names of entities (e.g., *item*) are in italics.
Named attributes (e.g., "address") are in quotes.
Page numbers in boldface refer to figures.